THE
DISRUPTORS

THE
*DISRUPT*ORS

Social entrepreneurs *reinventing* business and society

KERRYN KRIGE AND GUS SILBER

Gordon Institute of Business Science
University of Pretoria

ISBN: 978-1-928257-17-2
e-ISBN: 978-1-928257-18-9

First edition, first impression 2016
Second impression 2016

Published by Bookstorm (Pty) Ltd on behalf of
the Gordon Institute of Business Science
26 Melville Road
Illovo
Johannesburg 2196
South Africa
www.gibs.co.za

Edited by Wesley Thompson
Proofread by Kelly Norwood-Young
Cover illustration by iStock/PsychoShadowMaker
Cover design by mr design
Book design and typesetting by mr design

FSC
Printed by ABC Press, Cape Town

CONTENTS

LIST OF ACRONYMS

ABCD	Asset-Based Community Development
ANC	African National Congress
BBA	Bachelor of Business Administration
CBD	Central Business District
CIDA	Community and Individual Development Association
COO	Chief Operating Officer
CSI	Corporate Social Investment
DA	Democratic Alliance
GDP	Gross Domestic Product
GIBS	Gordon Institute of Business Science
HERI	Helenvale Recycling Initiative
IDC	Industrial Development Corporation
IFP	Inkatha Freedom Party
ICEE	International Centre for Eyecare Education
MBA	Master of Business Administration
MEC	Member of the Executive Council
MMS	Multimedia Messaging Service
NGO	Non-Governmental Organisation
NPO	Non-Profit Organisation
PBO	Public-Benefit Organisation
SABC	South African Broadcasting Corporation
SME	Small to Medium-sized Enterprise
TM	Transcendental Meditation
UNICEF	United Nations Children's Fund
WEF	World Economic Forum

FOREWORD

In 2002 I joined the Schwab Foundation for Social Entrepreneurship and discovered, at the annual meeting in Davos, the world's largest network of social entrepreneurs – disruptors whose groundbreaking innovations have a widespread, positive social impact.

Over the years, I have observed a proliferation of best-practice social entrepreneurs emerge in Asia and Latin America, but only a trickle in Africa, despite the concept of ubuntu, which captures the heart of wanting to solve social issues. In 2005, Futhi Mtoba, then Chairperson of Deloitte in South Africa, herself a social entrepreneur and founder of TEACH South Africa, convened a national conference for social entrepreneurship, with the aim of identifying and recognising community-based South African social enterprises. Business, government, the media and the general public were invited, in the hope that they would embrace social entrepreneurs in our communities as another path to address the country's social challenges, and to talk about social entrepreneurship in development forums. Many local social entrepreneurs showcased their work at Gallagher Estate, Johannesburg. But business and government's response was disappointing.

Social entrepreneurship is not a cure-all for poverty. It cannot bridge the inequality gap and create employment on its own. Social enterprises cannot substitute state provision of healthcare, education, housing, sanitation, water, infrastructure, etc. They don't have sufficient resources and capacity to deliver these goods and services. Yet, social entrepreneurs provide within communities. They create employment, ensuring that low-income households can put food on their tables. They provide additional intervention strategies and give substance to the slogan "Together, we can do more". Therefore, their efforts should not be ignored.

Social entrepreneurs identified and showcased by the Schwab Foundation at the World Economic Forum (WEF) platforms, as well as Ashoka Fellows, participants in the Skoll World Forum on Social Entrepreneurship, and delegates of the Gordon Institute of Business Science (GIBS) Network for Social Entrepreneurs, attest to the many benefits that they have gained from structured learning, formal networking and interfacing with business leaders, investors and fellow social entrepreneurs.

GIBS, as an educational institution that has embraced the role of social entrepreneurship in development, is observing due diligence to new social-enterprise models in documenting their authenticity and showcasing them to the country and the world. In this important book, social entrepreneurs who are leading change in South Africa are showcased. It shows enormous progress from the early days of 2005, and our conversations at Gallagher Estate.

One such innovator who emerges from these pages is Pat Pillai, who considers himself to be essentially a teacher. Yet he plays in the global league, as does South Africa's Garth Japhet of Soul City, who for years has graced the Development Dialogues at Davos. Pat's Non-Profit Organisation (NPO) is called Life College. This book captures the journey of these entrepreneurial ventures, but, as Pat says, "You never really graduate from life. You just get better at dealing with it." Through challenges, Pat has grown his enterprise: "Today, it is not unusual for Life College, now known as LifeCo UnLtd, to be paid R5 million a year for a development programme for a school, university, or other organisation." But always, the contract is social. "The aim is to build a nation of champions."

Then there are star performers, such as Gregory Maqoma, the dancer whose financials, budgets, statements and expenses "are not the natural beat for a company of dancers", and innovators such as Jonathan Liebmann, who is transforming Johannesburg, aiming to make money while having a social impact. Liebmann believes that profits make enterprises more sustainable. He says, "That is the interesting thing for the social entrepreneur. Finding balance." Yes indeed!

We must include serial social entrepreneur, Thandazile Mary Raletooane, who is "haunted by the sights she has seen, of children tied up like animals and left in ramshackle shelters, victims of abuse and trauma". Yet, through her work, Thandazile has brought hope to her community. "Hope is what rolls up its sleeves and puts its hands to work…In work there is pride. In work there is dignity. In work there is the opportunity to turn disability into sustainability." Thandazile is a serial social entrepreneur, "not because she is building businesses, but because she is helping others to help others".

I believe we are at a tipping point, with excellent examples of organisations that demonstrate success in creating social and economic value. I hope that this book will inspire the South African business community to seek out and partner with these innovative enterprises, so that they become sustainable and replicable models, and so that government creates a conducive regulatory environment that will spur more citizens to innovate effective and scalable social enterprises.

GIBS, with its academic and executive programmes in social

entrepreneurship, and its networks, is the potential catalyst that we need in South Africa to bring big business, government and civil society together and to showcase South African entrepreneurs, similar to the annual global showcase of social entrepreneurs in Davos. The standard of South Africa's social entrepreneurs is comparable to their global counterparts, and they would benefit from the exposure, education and support that interaction with business and change-makers would bring, firmly establishing social entre-preneurship as a recognised and legitimate development intervention in our country. GIBS has an important leadership role to play in this respect.

Together, we can do more!

Zanele Mbeki
November 2015

INTRODUCTION

On the Flipside of Profit

The GIBS Network for Social Entrepreneurs published its first book on social entrepreneurship in 2007, entitled *From Dust to Diamonds: Stories of South African Entrepreneurs*, recognising the value that disruptors were creating in society, and exploring what the country's leading changemakers were doing. But by 2015, these stories were becoming dated, swept aside by a growing movement of citizens motivated not just by profit, but also by improving the country they live in. These citizens are all deeply connected to South Africa, recognising that the only way to improve the system is through direct action.

As I'm writing this introduction, the #FeesMustFall protests have swept across the country, with calls for equality, opportunity, and choice for young people. This is the consequence of years of a growing inequality between rich and poor that has South Africa vying for top spot on the Gini index as the most unequal country in the world. Slow economic growth means we have a cohort of young people – who make up more than half of our population – facing a future with poor employment prospects. South Africa's reality is that 50 per cent of its young people are unemployed, and this is unlikely to change unless we disrupt the foundations of our society. Our education system is often ranked worst in the world, despite consistent investment by government that matches that of developed economies. It is a scenario that many African countries face, and the disruptors to this impasse are those who are able to create both social and economic change, particularly in communities that don't have easy access to markets or economies. These are our social entrepreneurs.

Social entrepreneurship has long been a confusing topic, with multiple interpretations and no wrong definitional answers. This was part of the reason for the genesis of this book: to deepen our understanding of social entrepreneurs in South Africa, to get a sense of who they are, where they work and what drives them. They are a wild and varied group, working in the arts, growing and selling seeds, developing computer games, making materials for contact lenses, teaching maths, linking rural communities.

Drawing these entrepreneurs together is a long view – they don't look at the gains of short-term profit, but rather value investing in and connecting people, networking communities that many have forgotten. Their altruism is not pity based; in fact, it disrupts our cultural sense of charity, and the Victorian concepts of philanthropy and giving alms to the poor. Because all of these disruptors earn income from their work, their organisations are sustainable, dependent on a mix of grant funding, commercial- and venture-capital loans, and profit earned through the work they do. This creates an interesting dynamic not present in the charity sector: because if the work that is delivered is not relevant or needed – i.e. if there is no impact – then there is no business. All of our social entrepreneurs have an inherent and clear understanding that impact is mutual, and earned.

As is the case with many great social ideas, this book started with frustration, and then foresight. My colleague, Itumeleng Dhlamini, who has been deeply involved in the book's production process, came upstairs to our offices, as a student of our social entrepreneurship programme, frustrated that we didn't have a textbook that captured the diversity and value of today's social entrepreneurs. Without her frustration and foresight, this book would be waiting for someone else's frustration and foresight to happen. From there, with the support of the National Treasury and the Government of Flanders, we started exploring our landscape of social entrepreneurs. We placed adverts, started mining our network, and asked lots of questions. The end result is a collection of stories of people who identify, or who others have identified, as social entrepreneurs, and whose work gives depth to the realities of life in South Africa.

A short academic section is included at the end of each chapter to help readers, and teachers, flag why our social entrepreneurs are different – illustrating the choices they've had to make and how this compares with the experience of others. We have included a References and Further Reading list for those who want to know more about the academic literature, and we have created a website that includes videos and transcripts of the interviews with all of the social entrepreneurs, at www.leadingchange.co.za.

The book is divided into four parts.

The first part includes stories that give insight into the power and possibility of our social entrepreneurs – who are they? What do they do? What makes them different?

The second part tells stories that flag some of the character traits of social entrepreneurs – how do they think? What makes them see the world differently? What motivates them to focus on social change over profit?

The third part looks at social entrepreneurs and innovation, their navigation of unknown territory and their efforts to resolve the formidable tension that remains unresolved between earning a profit and focusing on change.

Finally, we have input from Brett Gilbert and Jeffrey Robinson, of Rutgers University, who provide deeper academic insight into South Africa's social entrepreneurs and how this connects to the international environment.

This book is meant to be a wonderful read, stimulating and thought-provoking – an insight that takes us past the media headlines of protest, systemic fracture and economic lethargy, to emphasise the disruptive opportunities that exist if we look beyond the typical ways of doing things. If we can see alternatives to the pure for-profit motive of business, and appreciate opportunities in our communities, if we focus on collaboration and not isolation – and the distinct value that collaboration generates – and if we can encourage the non-conformist spirit of the entrepreneur, we will quickly create a social *and* economic cohesiveness that underpins success.

I hope you read this book multiple times, in many locations. Share it. Bend the spine. Dog-ear the pages you want to reread. Leave it in the kitchen to browse when a pot of something is simmering on the stove. Leave it on the train. Give it to your taxi driver. This book is to be read and shared, and I hope it encourages you to see the enormous opportunities that exist on the flipside of profit.

Kerryn Krige
November 2015

DREAMING AND DISRUPTING: THE POWER OF SOCIAL ENTREPRENEURSHIP

LUDWICK MARISHANE

THE EUREKA MOMENT OF LUDWICK MARISHANE

Spurred into invention by a casual remark from a teenage school friend, a young Limpopo entrepreneur learns the business value of bathing without bathing

Archimedes, in Ancient Greece, sank into his bath, deep in thought. Buoyed by the warm and soothing water, he mulled over the weight on his mind. A challenge from a king: figure out whether a goldsmith was short-changing the royal crown by sneaking silver threads amongst the gold. Archimedes, the renowned scientist and mathematician, lay back, the wavelets lapping over the edge. Then he sat up with a splash. All he had to do, he realised, was dunk the crown in water, and measure the volume of its displacement. He leaped from the bath and ran naked down the street, proclaiming his epiphany to the world. "Eureka! Eureka!" *I have found it.*

A couple of thousand years later, in the dry and dusty village of Motetema in Limpopo, South Africa, a young man named Ludwick Marishane – scholar by profession, entrepreneur by aspiration – was lazing in the winter sunshine with his friend, Kholofelo. They were sunbathing, and their talk meandered to bathing, and what a chore it was on a bitterly cold night, when you had to stand shivering while your mom poured boiling water from the kettle into the tub. Ludwick boasted that he could go for a week without taking a bath, and smell just as pleasant, thanks to the miracle of his metabolism. The only way his mom could tell he hadn't bathed was by the sweat stains on his clothes.

This made Kholofelo wonder: "Why can't someone invent something that you can just put on your skin, and then you wouldn't need to take a bath at all?" Ludwick's eyes lit up. This was it. This was the Big Idea he had been searching for. Instant success: just subtract water. "Man," said Ludwick to his pal, "I would buy that."

Ever since his father had given him a chemistry kit for his tenth birthday, Ludwick had wanted to be a scientist, an inventor of things. Once, he ingested copper sulphate by mistake, and his face swelled up like a balloon, and he had to be rushed to hospital. But what is science, other than a process of learning through trial and error?

Still in high school, Ludwick was a natural tinkerer, an "intentrepreneur",

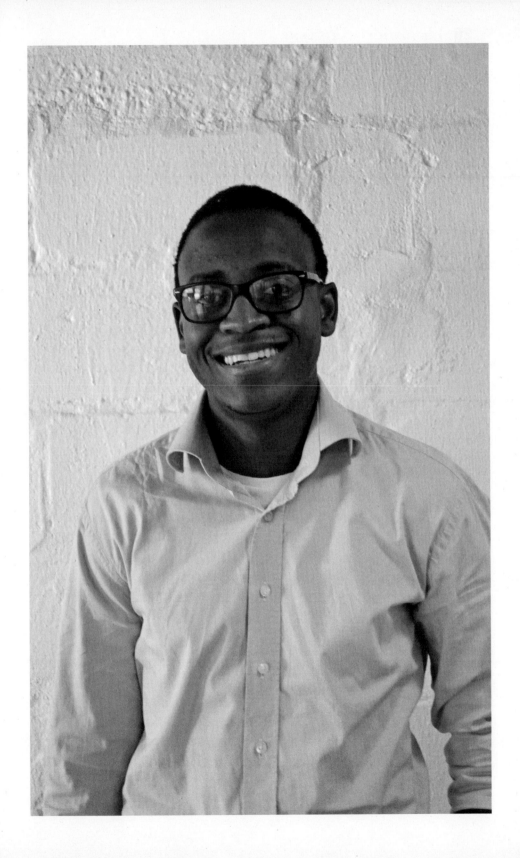

brimful of business ideas that he toyed and grappled with and push-started to the brink of possibility. His grand ambition was to be a billionaire by the age of 25. His lesser ambition was to change the world. He had tried his hand at formulating diesel biofuel from algae, but put it on the back-burner when he was beaten to the punch by a big firm with government funding of R50 million. He didn't have that kind of money. Then, trying to tap into the massive global market for antidotes to smoking, he hand-rolled a "healthy cigarette" from the leaves of *Camellia sinensis*, a shrub used to make green tea. He asked a few friends to light up and take a puff. "It tastes crap," they said. So he put a hold on that too.

Now, lolling in the sun in Limpopo, his neurons were firing as he raced through the permutations. Waterless bathing. How many people in the world would be in the market for that? Soldiers in battle, patients in hospital, outdoor adventurers, athletes, airline passengers, business travellers, field workers and explorers, campers and festival-goers, long-distance drivers, lazy teenage boys by the million. When the body is at rest, the mind is in motion, and here it led Ludwick on a journey from idea to activation, from the glimmer of a prospect to a product with global reach and purpose. DryBath.

> His grand ambition was to be a billionaire by the age of 25. His lesser ambition was to change the world.

When people speak of the Great South African Innovations – the first human heart transplant, the automatic pool cleaner, the concrete breakwater shaped like an ox's knucklebone – they may want to add the outcome of Ludwick's eureka moment to the list. It epitomises the ethos of *'n Boer maak 'n plan*: a quick and dirty solution to a nagging problem. All right, a quick and clean solution. DryBath is a moisturising gel that you rub on your skin, from a bottle or a snap-open sachet, to keep you fresh and clean when you can't or don't want to take a bath. For the founder and Managing Director of Headboy Industries Inc., the company that developed and manufactures DryBath, this is big business with a social imperative.

More than two-and-a-half billion people do not have proper access to water and sanitation, says Ludwick, leaving them open to such debilitating conditions as cholera, dysentery, and trachoma, an infection spread by flies attracted to moist eyes on dirty faces. As he told the audience at a TED Talk in Johannesburg, "Even if I'm not just doing it for myself and the fact that I don't want to bathe, I at least need to do it to try to save the world." But DryBath is a commercial product, and Headboy Industries is a for-profit enterprise, funded organically from private savings and the winnings from business-plan competitions.

Ludwick's business partner, who holds a 25 per cent stake, is Dr Hennie du Plessis, a chemical engineer and packaging mastermind whose own eureka moment came during a struggle with a fast-food hamburger and a messy, hard-to-open sachet of tomato sauce. He invented a technology called Easysnap: a rigid sachet with butterfly wings that you squeeze to get the goo out. Ludwick learned about the invention online, and went to see Hennie at his factory in Somerset West. Hennie had worked in the armaments industry before going out on his own to market a more effective ultrasound gel he had developed. Ludwick was impressed by Hennie's entrepreneurial drive, as much as by his versatility as a scientist. Rather than just supply the packaging, Hennie formulated the product too, from a combination of essential oils, deionised water, table salt, and acids.

"We have never taken an equity investment," says Ludwick. "We have never taken anyone's money. I don't believe in charity or donations." At the same time, while he resists the notion that he is a social entrepreneur in the conventional sense, he believes there should be a limit on how much entrepreneurs can earn through their corporate structures. "In the same way that there is limited downside risk," he says, "companies should have limited upside reward."

For now, the social imperative of DryBath is to turn the tap firmly to the right. Each DryBath Moment, as Ludwick calls it, saves 40 litres of water. Per month, based on online sales of 5,000 units, that's 20,000 litres of water saved. In three months, you'll have saved enough water to fill a typical sub-urban swimming pool. Given the potential applications for the technology, that figure may seem like a drop in the ocean. But it is testimony to the challenges of scale, pricing, and distribution that bedevil every entrepreneur who has dared to take a bright idea to market.

For every breakthrough, every landmark achievement – Ludwick is South Africa's youngest patent holder, a Google EMEA Campus Ambassador, a winner of multiple scholarships, and the first African to be declared a Global Student Entrepreneur of the Year – there has been an obstacle, a setback, a missed opportunity. Ludwick was in his third year of a business science degree at the University of Cape Town, running his company on the side, studying until 1 or 2 am, when a R30-million distribution deal with an Indian company fell through over a deadlock on the price of DryBath.

"They wanted to sell that sachet, which is enough for your whole body, for R1 in India," says Ludwick. "We had no capacity to produce the sachets cheaper than R1 each, even if they bought all of the three million sachets we were producing a month. They were not willing to budge on the packaging in order to achieve the required cost savings." While the deal would have stabilised Ludwick's startup, he ended the negotiations after three months because it would have meant competing on price, rather than on product quality. "The goal of a business is to become as natural a monopoly as possible," says Ludwick, "not to worry about how to be cheaper than their competition." Still, he couldn't help thinking about the money. "I was like, no! I lost out on a R30-million opportunity. But I had school to worry about. I had to fit in meetings at night, because during the day I had to go to class. Nothing was working out."

He thought about dropping out, reasoning that "nobody who makes a billion ever finishes university while they are making a billion", but he stayed the course and graduated business science with Honours.

In the real world, if you want to make it as an entrepreneur, you master failure and disappointment. You take the hard knocks as they come, and you figure out a way to spring back on your feet, shrugging and laughing. Ludwick, smart-casual in mustard jeans and a pale-blue shirt with the sleeves crumpled up, has an easygoing charm, his eyes alive with curiosity and mischief. He has the quality of "swag": the cool confidence that comes from knowing you're doing something you love, even when it hurts. But swag is also part hustle, part bluster, part thinking on your feet, as Ludwick illustrates when he tells a story about the early days of DryBath, before he enlisted Hennie du Plessis to give form and substance to his invention.

> He has the quality of "swag": the cool confidence that comes from knowing you're doing something you love, even when it hurts. But swag is also part hustle, part bluster, part thinking on your feet.

He had a formula, a prototype, a brand, a business plan, a proposition – "DryBath is a rich man's convenience and a poor man's lifesaver" – but what he didn't have was a product he could show off to prospective buyers. He was invited to take part in a showcase at a water conference at the V&A Waterfront in Cape Town. His business partner at the time, Keoikantse Marungwana, an engineering Masters student at the University of Cape Town, said, so what are we going to showcase? Ludwick laughs. "If there is anything I have learned from the big boys, Steve Jobs, Bill Gates and those guys, it's that they all bluffed their way when they didn't have the thing. I said, look, we will go to Clicks, buy a couple of hand sanitisers, take off the labels, and put on our own labels. We already know that most people are averse to the idea, so nobody is going to want to take it home and try it, but they will use it on their hands and say it smells nice or whatever." As it turned out, he needn't have bothered. "There was no conversion," says Ludwick. "It was a waste of time. We got all the typical reactions. 'It isn't going to work. It's great for poor people, but I wouldn't use it.' So we just continued."

The partnership came to an end when Keoikantse left to join the corporate world after completing his degree, but Ludwick had learned a valuable lesson about business. Showing up is all very well, but sooner or later, you have to come up with the goods. The best advice he got back then was from a team at Union Swiss, a skincare multinational with offices in Long Street, Cape Town. He had won an Allan Gray scholarship to study at the University of Cape Town, and he had met them at a networking event. It was his first formal business meeting. He wore a business suit, on a seething-hot day, and when he arrived, "there were these guys wearing holiday pants and holiday shirts and flip-flops. I am new to the game, so I am like, what? Nice to be the boss." The first thing they said to Ludwick, looking at his formula for DryBath, was, why do you think nobody has already done this? "There is nothing unique. There is no new, invented ingredient in your product. You are using common ingredients, so if someone goes and re-engineers it, what do you do?" Just build the brand, they said. Get it out to the people. See if it works. That's how you do it. He was like a sponge, absorbing information and wisdom wherever he could.

The question, at this point, arises: why would you want to use DryBath if you could just use hand sanitiser? The simple answer is that hand sanitiser is for hands. It is too harsh to use on the face or elsewhere on the body. Ludwick learned this, and plenty more, on his personal crash course on gels and lotions, thumbing his way through Google and Wikipedia on his trusty Nokia 6234, soon after that conversation with his high school pal, Kholofelo.

Ludwick is a case study in the power of the mobile phone as a tool of empowerment and enlightenment for the African entrepreneur. Without access to a computer, he used his Nokia to research the skincare industry, download a patent and formula for hand sanitiser, and tap-type a 40-page business plan in Multimedia Messaging Service (MMS), limited to 1,000 characters at a time. He copied and pasted the document bit by bit into Gmail, emailed it to himself, and printed it out at an internet café. He saw it as a creative exercise, akin to his other obsession, composing rap songs and setting them to a beat. He was the hip-hop guy, in his bandana, flat cap, and low-slung trousers.

In his mid-20s, Ludwick is young enough to be able to pinpoint, with surgical precision, the moment he became the Cool Kid in Class. It was one of those lessons: a lucky break that taught him the importance of finding your direction in life. His father, Stanford Malatji, an HR executive, once said,

"Ludwick, what side of the road do people drive on?" It was a trick question for the eight-year old. "I didn't pay attention," says Ludwick. "I said, well, when I go to school, I am on the left-hand side, and when I come back, I am on the right-hand side." One day, he was crossing the road in a rush, to catch a taxi home from school. He didn't look left, and he didn't see the car that smashed into him. He was off school for a month. "It was so cool. I was the kid with the broken leg. I think that is how I finally melded with everyone. It was something weird we could all talk about."

Before that, he was the misfit, the outsider, the Sepedi-speaking kid from deep-rural Limpopo, battling to cross the barriers of language and culture at a Model-C school in the suburb of Highlands North, Johannesburg. His parents had separated, and he had moved to the city to live with his father. On his first day at school, he bought a hamburger with his tuckshop money. "This girl comes up to me, I think she was in Grade 3 or 4, and she says, how much was the burger? I had no idea what she was saying, so I just stared at her and said, 'How much.' She said again, how much was the burger? And I said, 'How much.' She eventually just walked away. That conversation has always stuck with me."

But he was a quick and bright learner, a traveller between worlds, flitting from his father's home in Johannesburg to the home of his mother, Lovemore Marishane, in Limpopo, and it wasn't long before he learned the meaning of how much. "I have been the CEO of my own education since Grade 2," says Ludwick. Every evening at 7 pm, his father would sit him down and listen to him reporting on his learnings of the day. "What I learned before break time, what I learned after break, what I learned after school, if I did all my homework, and so on. He did it religiously every day. I don't know where he learned it from, because he grew up without a father. I was just like, why do I have to do this? All my friends go home and they watch TV and life goes on. Why do I have to do all this stuff?" The learning was its own answer.

He was an A student, top of his class, and by the time he got to high school, Maryvale College in Johannesburg, he was questioning even the most basic precepts of the system. One day, in religious studies class, he said to his teacher, "I don't buy this. This stuff does not make sense to me." In the uproar of that moment, he realised that heresy lies not in the questions you ask, but in the fact that you are asking questions. "I actively took on this persona of no, you really need to poke at things to see if they are what they say they are," he says. "You can't just take it for granted. I became comfortable with the fact that I could go and figure things out for myself, rather than just have an answer handed to me and take it as truth." The sceptical mind, the maverick attitude. Essential skills for an entrepreneur in the making.

But Ludwick, the Cool Kid in the Class, was picking up other skills too. Strategic thinking, rigorous planning, audacious tactical opportunism, the careful calculation of risk versus reward. In other words, he had what it took to be a kleptomaniac. At school, he had a brief but busy side career as a "negative entrepreneur", a scheming miscreant who turned to petty crime out of boredom and teenage mischief. He once led a raid on a soccer pitch to steal a goalpost to use for basketball. But the really big job, the one that most taught him a lesson about choices in business and life, was the tuckshop heist. The cash was in the till, right where you could see it. The tuckshop was locked between breaks. The key was on a hanger, just behind the receptionist. "I don't remember how we managed to distract her, but we stole the key, made a copy, and dropped it off the next day. I think they had a spare, so nobody noticed anything." The heist, small amounts at a time, ran for about two weeks, before the lock was changed. "The books obviously were not adding up," says Ludwick. "So we said, stop while you are ahead. For me it was evidence that if you set your mind to doing something, you can actually get it done, regardless of whether it is legal or illegal. To me, it proves that my brain could have taken a different path. I could have become a criminal mastermind, instead of a business person."

> "If you set your mind to doing something, you can actually get it done, regardless of whether it is legal or illegal. To me, it proves that my brain could have taken a different path. I could have become a criminal mastermind, instead of a business person."

The line is fine. It is a lesson he wants to share with the world. The better path leads towards the things you dream. He is a long way, still, from being a billionaire: "My friends know how broke I am," he says. "I haven't even built my mom a house yet." But he has managed to build a business on the premise of a throwaway joke, with a product that holds the power to make a difference to people's lives. Eureka.

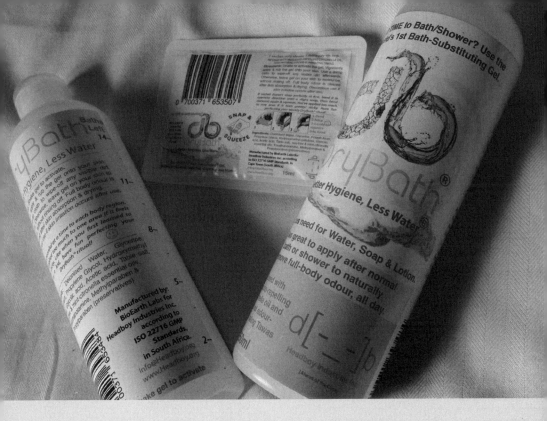

Big Business with a Social Imperative

Austin, Stevenson and Wei-Skillern's (2006) article, "Social and Commercial Entrepreneurship: Same, Different, or Both?" poses a question that applies to Ludwick: is he a for-profit entrepreneur who has spotted his opportunity in a social context, or, because he sees opportunity in the constraint of his context, is he a social entrepreneur?

Austin et al. (2006) compare the dimensions of opportunity, context, people, resources and deals for social and commercial entrepreneurs. Where the two types diverge is in context: whereas the social entrepreneur chooses to operate in an adverse context (because this is where social value will be found), the commercial entrepreneur looks for opportunity in an opportunity-rich environment. Both rely on people and resources to access networks, funds and influence, but the social entrepreneur operates in an inherently resource-constrained environment and often cannot access commercial funds unless they set up a separate for-profit entity.

A Basic Need in One Market, a Luxury in Another

The commercial entrepreneur spots opportunities in new needs, or in breakthrough ways to meet existing needs, whereas the social entrepreneur focuses on meeting basic needs. In contrast to commercial entrepreneurs, social entrepreneurs conduct deals, exchanges of value, across complex dimensions of type, consumers, timing, flexibility and measurability (Austin et al., 2006).

Ludwick is both a commercial and a social entrepreneur. DryBath meets a basic need in one market and a luxury need in another, and as a result he works in adverse and opportunity-rich contexts. Because of the social nature of his work and the for-profit structure of his business, he can access resources through both commercial and grant funding, but has chosen to focus on utilising income and personal investments, to finance the business. His deals are therefore commercial – the more he sells, the more he can grow his business. And the more he sells into water-scarce areas, the greater the impact of his work, adding to the complexity of his deal value.

Austin et al., (2006) place social and commercial entrepreneurship on opposite ends of a continuum, recognising that the purest for-profit business has social elements, and vice versa. The model opposite adapts Sahlman's framework of entrepreneurship (cited in Austin et al., 2006) and plots Ludwick's work on the continuum, using the criteria of People, Context, Deal and Opportunity.

Social entrepreneurs focus on providing social value through deals, operating with constrained access to people and resources, and in adverse contexts. The major source of opportunity for the social entrepreneur is in providing for basic needs.

On the opposite end of the continuum, the commercial entrepreneur looks for commercial value in deals, is highly networked, has access to resources and talent, and works in an advantageous context, responding to opportunities to provide for new/breakthrough needs.

So, is Ludwick a social entrepreneur? He does not regard himself as one, but when plotted on the spectrum, he is a blend of both: "big business with a social imperative".

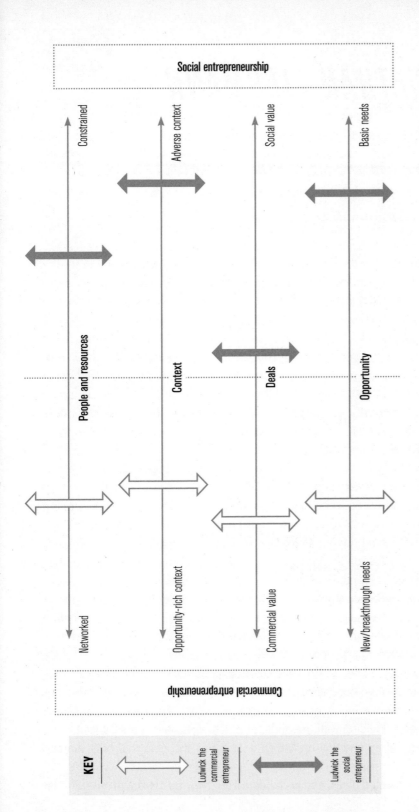

Ludwick plotted on the People, Context, Deals and Opportunities framework presented as a spectrum from commercial to social entrepreneurship

Model based on the PCDO triangle and Sahlman's framework of social entrepreneurship from Austin et al, 2006

JONATHAN LIEBMANN

THE MAVERICK OF MABONENG

Living and working in the heart of the city he is helping to define, Jonathan Liebmann is driven by a dream of renewal and transformation in Johannesburg's bustling Place of Light

Johannesburg was born in dust and chaos, stirred by a stampede for the gold that lay buried in the rock. From afar came the miners, the prospectors, the fortune seekers, the hunters of opportunity and the hustlers of hope. They're still here.

One Sunday morning, just off Main Street on the east side of town, a car stands draped with colourful clothing, tee shirts and kaftans hooked on netting, sandals and baskets displayed on the roof. On the pavement, a busker strums a guitar, competing with the putt-putt of a tuk-tuk picking up a passenger. A little further on, at Arts on Main, a gravel-crunchy courtyard offers space to pause amidst the bustle, before you cross the portal into the maze of the food and craft market.

Here, chickpeas on the sizzle in a cast-iron pan; there, the sweet jolt of a giant red-velvet cupcake; and here, on the wall of a boutique at the top of the fire escape, a souvenir keyrack in the shape of a familiar silhouette: the skyline of a city, with towers like needles, skyscrapers like a bar chart, and the webbing of a bridge peeking up like a yacht on the waves.

"Love Jozi", reads the label, and this place offers reason enough to obey that gentle command. From the swoop of the freeway flyover, with its concrete struts decked in bold, bright street art, the district of Maboneng radiates like the meaning of its Sesotho name, the Place of Light, illuminating a part of the city that is being redefined, redeveloped, and rejuvenated for a new generation of city-goers and city-stayers.

Maboneng is lofts and galleries, coffeeshops and craft factories, studios and markets, workshops, restaurants, and a 12-room hotel, each artfully decorated room chronicling a decade in the life of the city. And here, on Fox Street, in a facebrick building with the ghost of a 7Up logo on its gable, it is also the hub of an entrepreneurial dream, as enticing as the gold that built the city. Let's take the stairs.

They're painted black, and each bears a buzzword, a mantra of mission, that

catches your eye and beckons you to a higher level. Independence, Passion, Teamwork, Creativity, Respect, Innovation, Initiative, Extreme Optimism, Diligence, Results, Moxie, Accountability, Integrity. At the top of the stairs, stands Jonathan Liebmann.

He is wearing black jeans and an untucked shirt with rolled-up sleeves, revealing bracelets on one wrist and a watch on the other. His collar-length hair is swept back, and the stubble on his face suggests a man who is both on trend and too busy to shave. He is in his early 30s.

Jonathan is the founder and CEO of Propertuity, an inner-city property development firm whose name alone confirms that essential Johannesburg quality of moxie, the brazen confidence to kick-start a venture that is designed to linger in all perpetuity.

Every city is subject to change, in the way it looks and the way it works, the way it shakes off its dust and slaps on a new coat of paint. But beyond the surface, Johannesburg is pulsing with a revolution in urban renewal, from warehouses reimagined as open-plan markets (The Sheds@1Fox) to parking lots repurposed as farmers' markets (Neighbourgoods) to vibrant precincts of culture, community, and learning (Newtown).

> "We're literally building a city," says Jonathan, a born Johannesburger, whose heart beats quicker beneath the diamond-blue sky.

The Propertuity model of urban regeneration has equally found a home in Durban, the balmy coastal city where Jonathan grew up. Here, beginning with a weekly marketplace and office space for entrepreneurs in the once run-down Rivertown precinct in Morrison Street, he has begun laying the groundwork for what he calls "a culturally rich and urban Durban".

For now, Maboneng is the most ambitious of these initiatives, built on a mixed-use model of retail, residential, and industrial, with tired old buildings transformed into fresh new spaces, landscaped and styled with theatrical flair. "We're literally building a city," says Jonathan, a born Johannesburger, whose heart beats quicker beneath the diamond-blue sky, famous for distilling heat and electricity into drenching, dramatic storms in summer. It was that natural energy, that hint of danger in the air, that drew Jonathan back from a quieter life in London, where he took on odd jobs – construction, telesales – after a school career distinguished mostly by his casual absence from classes.

"It was one of those schools," he says, referring to Crawford College, a private institution that places independence and free thinking high on the curriculum. "Nobody knew." He learned more from his father, Benji, a lawyer turned banker turned patron of the arts, and his mother, Marilyn, a fashion designer turned entrepreneur. He was born in Johannesburg, but lived in Durban until the age of 15, when he returned to Joburg.

"I probably became a typical badly behaved teenager from about 13. I became quite rebellious. Before that, I was a much more diligent child. At 15, I moved to Johannesburg and started doing different business things." Right from the start, his Big Thing was property. He was still a teenager when he bought a ramshackle apartment in the suburb of Waverley, with his business partner's father standing surety. It cost him R270,000. He fixed it up, and sold it for a tidy profit. He put some of his earnings into a coffeeshop on wheels, Caffe Pronto, moving from market to market, getting a feel for the buzz of the city and giving the city a buzz in return.

He studied business and accounting at Monash in Johannesburg, a satellite campus of a Melbourne-based university. "It was small," he says, "so I was able to manipulate the vibe to my liking. I didn't actually go to university at all. I just went to write the exams." As part of his course, he dreamed up an enterprise called Daily Maid, theorising that there might be a market for the cleaning of apartments and homes on contract. He turned his assignment into a real business, but when it proved "too labour-intensive", he did what all fledgling entrepreneurs must do: he shifted gear and diversified, staying in the cleaning lane, but leaving the hard work to a crew of machines. Sorted.

That was the name of his chain of laundromats, which grew to 17, with the backing of a private investor. "It was not a good business," says Jonathan. He had a grand vision of building the biggest chain of laundromats in the country, but he lacked the appetite, the passion, to pursue it, because the truth is, he didn't do laundry. "I have still never ironed a shirt in my life," he says. "I just felt, I can't do anything like that. So how can I create a business and not know how it works? You should do something you are passionate about."

He admits, as an early starter, that he has rushed impulsively into the wrong sort of ventures, and that his drive to succeed has been tempered by indiscipline and a maverick streak. But here, at the intersection of bricks and mortar and the heartbeat of his home city, Jonathan has found his passion in a place of light.

Even the most faithful of Johannesburg's defenders would find it hard to argue that this is a conventionally beautiful metropolis. In place of mountains, it has toxic loaves of yellow sand upturned from the deep. In place of rivers, it has murky streams that slither through parkland and stagnate in freeway underpasses. In place of magnificent cathedrals, it has massive shopping malls. Even the most striking of the city's natural features, its swathes of urban forest, has its roots in a mandate to grow timber for the mines. But what Johannesburg does have is a pulse, a restless, defiant pride in its own pragmatism, its ability to find and bring the hidden beauty to light.

For Jonathan, Maboneng is a place to ignite that spirit, jump-start that energy, inject it with the adrenaline of life in the inner-city, the nucleus of the old and the new Johannesburg. In his gap year in London and the capitals of Europe, he was struck by the way cities connect people and people connect cities. They are organisms that thrive on symbiosis.

But Johannesburg, through the artifice of apartheid, was a city that prised people apart, that disconnected and alienated them from each other. Here, he says, "people live weird lives, suburban lives. There is no integration of people connecting in the street. Mainly, people live private lives."

Maboneng is a portfolio of properties, connected and integrated, assembled and redeveloped with profit and perpetuity in mind. But it is also a social experiment, a conduit to the human heart of Johannesburg. In that way, says Jonathan, mulling over the question, he may well qualify as a social entrepreneur, albeit as a byproduct of his motive to make money. "My position is, I want to make money and I want to make a positive impact. I think that we are transforming the city. That is our mandate. And I believe that the profits make it much more sustainable. That is the interesting thing for the social entrepreneur. Finding the balance."

Propertuity is funded by private equity, from the same silent partner who backed Jonathan's chain of laundromats, and loans from big financial institutions. The company, set up in 2007, employs more than 50 people, and has created more than 1,000 indirect jobs through outsourcing and satellite opportunities. But the founder himself isn't on the payroll. "I literally don't take money out, ever," says Jonathan. The profits he ploughs back into the business are meant to help it grow, and push his parallel agenda of social change. Five or ten years down the line, he concedes, he might want to shift the yin and yang a little. "It will be interesting to see what happens to my balance," he says. "What happens when there is R1 billion in the bank account? Because then you could go either way. You could say, I want more money, or you could say, a billion is enough and I want more social."

Johannesburg is an economy of intersections, between the have-lots and the have-nots, the gated suburbs and the informal settlements, the scrabblers for change at the traffic lights and the drivers in fast cars racing by. But the delicate shift, the twitch of the pressure gauge, lies somewhere between fear and hope. The fear is that systems will collapse, that infrastructure and basic services – electricity, transport, water – will fail under the weight of demand, that the city will one day fall to ruin.

For Jonathan, hope is on the rise. He lives on the 15th floor of a rede-signed office block in Maboneng, where the view he commands is of a city that must strive, higher and higher, to reach the sky. The future is vertical. He knows exactly what he would do if he was the Mayor of Johannesburg. He would put a moratorium on horizontal development, the sprawl of megacities and megasuburbs, spreading like lava on the fringes of the freeways. "Up, up, up," he says. "It's the only way. That is why New York, Tokyo, and Hong Kong work. They are islands. You can only go up. You can control electricity, water, and sanitation. This is the only answer here. Stop going horizontal."

He sleeps well at night. He feels safe. He lives and works and dreams inside the factory, the hub where things happen, the heart of the city. He wants to see Johannesburg become a place of mixed-use and mixed-income; poor people living next to rich people; a planned city, a normal city. Twenty years ago, he says, the Central Business District (CBD) of Johannesburg was at its worst: dangerous, poorly serviced, left almost derelict by the flight of business to the suburbs. "On a scale of one to ten, it was a one. Now, no one is going to argue if you say it's a three. When it gets to a five or a six, everyone is going to want to jump on the bandwagon. That is when people will begin to think that there is more good than bad in this place."

Jonathan sees himself as a strategist, not a manager. His driving impulse is design, not control. By nature, he is an outsider, an upstream swimmer, trying to figure things out for himself, because there is no template for what he is doing.

Jonathan sees himself as a strategist, not a manager. His driving impulse is design, not control. By nature, he is an outsider, an upstream swimmer, trying to figure things out for himself, because there is no template for what he is doing. "I have some people around me who can give me bits of advice," he says, "but they are not people who have been in this trajectory. High growth, fast. It is a problem for me. And I don't like those entrepreneurial organisa-tions that ask you to be part of them. I don't like being part of groups."

He has come to realise that entrepreneurship is a lonely business, and that growth and success are waypoints, not destinations. You have to keep on driving, faster and further, burning money on the route to making money. Cash flow is a funny thing, he says. No matter how well you plan, your projections are almost never right. "If you are growing a lot, that is the risk. It almost never happens that whatever you have provided for is R10 million better. It is always

R10 million worse. That is something I am still coming to terms with. You just have to have a healthy amount of, what do they call it, savings or liquidity."

But in Maboneng, he has found his purpose as well as his passion. He is defined by the city he is helping to define: creative, impatient, hungry, a little irascible but welcoming and warm at heart. He is shaping a small part of the skyline, the silhouette of the Jozi he knows and loves. The sounds rise up from the city street, the hubbub of music and chatter, the noise of traffic and shouting. The market is abuzz with commerce, industry, and ideas, the age-old brickwork splashed anew with colour and art.

The rush that built this city, on the cusp of the 19th Century, was a rush that drew people down into darkness, into the grip of the ore. Now there is a new hope, a new space, a new opportunity. Jonathan Liebmann, Mabonenger, Joburger, entrepreneur, lifts his eyes, up, up, up, and into the light.

INNOVATION
RESPECT
CREATIVITY
TEAMWORK
PASSION

The Positive Consequences of Social Entrepreneurship

Jonathan Liebmann is not an obvious social entrepreneur. Driven by a desire to make money in a sector that has inherent social value – providing houses and marketplaces for people – he is an example of the balancing act between social gain and profit. "My position is, I want to make money and I want to make a positive impact. I think that we are transforming the city. That is our mandate. And I believe that the profits make it much more sustainable. That is the interesting thing for the social entrepreneur. Finding the balance," Jonathan says. But his story tells of someone who saw opportunity in decay and who has subsequently grown a business based on a deep appreciation of regeneration and rejuvenation.

Jonathan is not your stereotypical commercial property developer. He fits Santos's (2012) positive theory of social entrepreneurship that argues that social entrepreneurs step into the spaces left by market failure – when government and businesses fail to provide services and support that they are mandated to, either because they can't, it is not in their interests to, or they are not best placed to (Krige, 2015). This is typically the domain of civil society – to plug the societal gaps – but it is the social entrepreneur who founds the organisation that does this with a for-profit focus, resulting in a positive consequence (Krige, 2016).

To Build a City is to Take the Long View

Santos argues that social entrepreneurship is the "pursuit of sustainable solutions, to neglected problems with positive externalities" (Santos, 2012, p. 335). Liebmann does this well: he has a long view – "We're literally building a city" – that has a permanence in an inner-city that exhibits all the signs of failure, which Bremner (2000) described as "diseased, crime-ridden, dangerous and disordered" (p. 191). Santos (2012) finds that social entrepreneurs are able to apply their model elsewhere, shifting from a local context to a regional and at times global relevance. Again, Liebmann fits the descriptor, as he works to replicate his Johannesburg model of development in the coastal city of Durban.

Santos distinguishes between social enterprises and other for-profit organisations by their approach to value: social enterprises create value, while typical for-profits capture value. According to Santos, social enterprises create value that can be measured in its utility, after costs, to members of society. Social entrepreneurs focus on positive systemic change, and based on this definition, Jonathan Liebmann is a social entrepreneur. Similarly, all organisations that have an inherent social impact in their work – hospitals, universities, private healthcare providers – would qualify as social enterprises, as long as value is reinvested in the social project, rather than extracted organisationally, individually or by external shareholders.

The model opposite illustrates the principles of the theory: that the identity of the social enterprise is created by a conscious decision to create rather than capture value. This value is created at a societal level, where value capture benefits the organisation or individual. Most businesses are in a constant cycle of trade-offs between value capture and creation but the social enterprise is distinct because value creation is its primary goal.

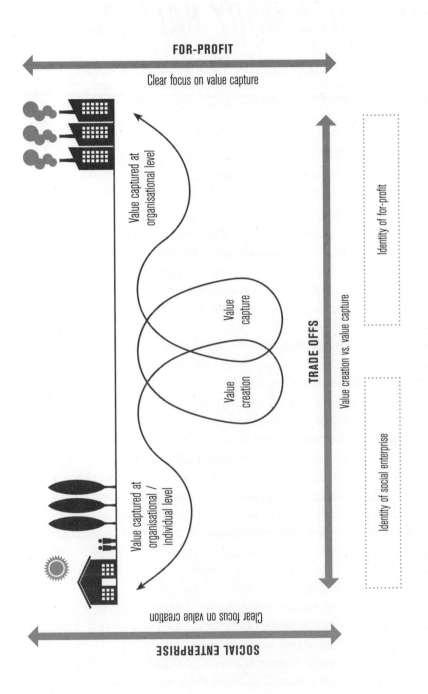

Social enterprises create rather than capture value
Adapted from Santos, 2012

THANDAZILE MARY RALETOOANE

A MOTHER OF THE NATION IN A PLACE OF NEGLECT

In a place known for suffering and neglect, Thandazile Mary Raletooane has put her heart and soul into creating jobs for women, and building a place of hope and care for orphaned and vulnerable children

The road is a flat line that cuts through the heart of the country, bypassing fields of maize where the windmills stand tall. In the distance is the ripple of the mountains, like waves, receding, beneath a diamond-blue sky. The beaten track of the R26, punched by potholes, is patched here and there by fresh hot tar, before the roaring pantechnicons spit up the gravel and rip up the old wounds all over again. But the scenery is beautiful, and it puts you in a Free State of mind.

The crags loom larger now, trees crowding the verge, as the town of Ficksburg beckons. A meander down shady streets, past gracious old buildings with corrugated-iron roofs and façades of local sandstone, glowing in the afternoon light. Every year, there is a cherry festival here, a celebration of the harvest in the heartland of Platteland hospitality. But if you carry on driving, to the edge of town, in the cradle of the Caledon River and the Maluti Range of neighbouring Lesotho, you will find yourself in a different state of mind.

In the topography of apartheid, every small town would have its township, an area of catchment and overspill, sited close enough to serve as a labour pool, and far enough to be out of sight and mind. In Ficksburg, that township is Meqheleng. It lies on a hilltop, overlooking the town, but the grimness of everyday life here mocks the lofty heights it commands. In narrow, unpaved streets, waste flows from burst pipes, and rubbish clogs the culverts after the rains. There are schools, clinics, small businesses, and a sports centre, but the township is best known as the home of Andries Tatane, a teacher and political activist, who was beaten and shot to death in clashes with police during protests over service delivery in 2011.

The name of the township alone is a political statement, a plea for help and redress. "*Meqheleng*" means "The Place of Neglect" in Sesotho. But for Thandazile Mary Raletooane, who has lived here all her life, neglect is not destiny. It is a spur to action.

Some know her as Mary, some prefer Thandazile, but she has come to be known by another name in these parts, an honorific she has earned by answering that call. Masechaba, the Mother of the Nation. If you were to ask for her in Meqheleng, you would be directed to the centre she runs as an NPO in Zone 2, with its sweeping views of the green valley and the flat-topped mountains beyond. The Itekeng Disabled Centre is a place of care and safety for orphaned and vulnerable children, and it also houses a wooden cabin where women sew clothes and make jewellery from beads, as part of a community job-creation project.

As nimble fingers string the bright baubles on strands of wire, Thandazile stands watching, her face aglow with pride. The sewing machines chatter, stitching swathes of patterned fabric into pretty clothes. It is just as Thandazile's grandmother used to say to her. If you want to make something out of life, you have to work hard. *Itekeng*. It means "help yourself". And if, in the process of helping yourself, you can help others, you are perpetuating the cycle of virtue that makes the world go round. You are making a meaningful difference.

> If, in the process of helping yourself, you can help others, you are perpetuating the cycle of virtue that makes the world go round. You are making a meaningful difference.

Outside, children run and play, past the white, tin-roofed building with the murals of smiling leaders, including Thandazile's two personal role models: Nelson Mandela, and Sefora Sisi Ntombela, the Member of the Executive Council (MEC) for Social Development in the Free State provincial government. Once, at a function during Child Protection Week, Thandazile stood up and asked the MEC if the government could please build a school for disabled children at her centre. The MEC said, but Ficksburg is a very small town. Thandazile explained that she was looking after 68 disabled children, and they could not stay in the same rooms as the able-bodied children in her care, because their health was so fragile. The MEC bowed her head for a moment. She looked up and said, "I am going to do it."

Three months went by. "I wrote emails to remind her," says Thandazile. "Just to say, MEC, I am just reminding you about this school. Last year she made a decision that she is going to build a school for Itekeng. This is the building they are doing." She points at the half-finished brick building, where workmen are carefully levelling the cement on the stairs. Sometimes, your hopes and dreams turn to bricks and mortar. You have to ask nicely, of the MEC and God – "*thandazile*" means "prayer" in Sesotho – and you have to remember what your grandmother said.

Her name was Selloane, and she single-handedly raised Thandazile and her siblings. She was a woman of strength and resolve, a fighter who got things done. If there was a crack in the wall, says Thandazile, her grandmother would mix sand, salt and water, and seal it herself. Thandazile was not just raised by her grandmother. She was uplifted. After completing her matric, she wanted to study to be a nurse, but the closest she got was working as a volunteer at a surgery in the town, where her sister was employed as a doctor's assistant. Thandazile would count pills and put them in their little envelopes, and she would call out the names of patients for their appointment with the doctor. In their suffering, she found her calling. She was not a nurse, but in her heart she was qualified to care, to ease the burden of those in pain and need.

Joining forces with ten other young people in Meqheleng, she started a hospice for HIV/Aids patients, in a building donated by the local Roman Catholic parish. "One day I was doing home-based care for a terminally ill patient," she says, "and that's when I saw three children staying by themselves in a shack. The oldest one was 13, and he had two siblings, one of three years and one of only eight months. They hadn't had any food for three weeks. We were crying that day."

It was a child-headed household, a sadly familiar consequence of the toll of HIV/Aids in South Africa. Thandazile arranged care for the children, taking the youngest into her own home. Moved by the plight of orphaned and vulnerable children, she heard about Itekeng. It was about to be closed by the provincial government.

"They didn't see progress, and there were only seven children," recalls Thandazile. She applied to work as a matron at the centre, confident that she would be able to use her natural organisational skills, her ability to evangelise a cause, to raise funds and awareness. She met with the management committee of Itekeng. One of the members, a teacher, said to her, you must go back to school, you are too young to work with disabled children.

"I said, it is my dream to work with children. I am not going to listen to this teacher. I am going forward, because God sent me here."

She went forward. She spoke to the business people of Meqheleng. Some donated money and clothing, some gave bread and milk and pledged to provide meals for the children. But the bigger challenge was convincing parents and the community that disabled children should be loved and looked after, not locked away and forgotten.

"Some people said that these children are possessed by the devil," says Thandazile. "I was trying to show them that this is not what the parents want their children to be. It is God's will. Ability is only temporary, and we must know that we are temporarily abled." Today Thandazile runs the centre with the help of volunteers, the support of doctors, nurses and physiotherapists, and funding from government and private donors. She calls Itekeng a place of hope and care, a haven for the outcasts, the neglected, and the vulnerable. She is haunted by the sights she has seen, of children tied up like animals and left in ramshackle shelters, victims of abuse and trauma.

"There are many things that make me sad," she says. One day, in the fierce heat of summer, she took a disabled child from the township into her care. "She was pregnant, and she didn't talk. She had been mistreated. When I asked the neighbours, they said, yes, we used to see the men who came here." There is another child, only 12 years old, who had been repeatedly raped by a man who would dress in women's clothing and pretend to be her mother. Thandazile was in court on the day the alleged rapist was appearing before the magistrate on a bail hearing. Thandazile stood up, shouting, and had to be restrained by police. The man did not get bail.

"Sometimes you don't want to talk to anyone," says Thandazile. "You just want to lock yourself away. I think what I must do with the people who are abusing…" She shakes her head. "I get so angry. I see it every day." But there is hope at Itekeng too. Hope is what rolls up its sleeves and puts its hands to work.

> But there is hope at Itekeng too. Hope is what rolls up its sleeves and puts its hands to work. In work there is pride. In work there is dignity. In work there is the opportunity to turn disability into sustainability.

The government grant for children in need ends on the day they turn 18, leaving Thandazile with a dilemma that cannot be solved by mere fundraising alone. In work there is pride. In work there is dignity. In work there is the opportunity to turn disability into sustainability.

Thandazile started a beadwork project. She took the finished crafts, the necklaces, bracelets and earrings, to the Ficksburg Cherry Festival, where they sold well. Her team of disabled crafters now also turns lumber from riverbank trees into woodwork, including chairs and, poignantly, coffins for children.

In Meqheleng, The Place of Neglect, Thandazile started a project called Itekeng Clean and Green, hiring young people, disabled people, and parents of disabled children, to keep the streets clean and the environment green. That has since grown into a full-scale Department of Public Works and Independent Development Trust contract, employing more than 700 people in five towns and surrounding farms. Each worker earns a nominal amount of up to R86 a day, depending on the season, a small seed of subsistence in a region rife with poverty.

She was thinking beyond her own town, her own centre, her own place in the world. She looked to the mountains, the sky and the river, and she saw that this was her home too. She felt a calling to look after it, and she couldn't do it alone. On a TV newscast one morning, Thandazile saw the Deputy Minister of Environmental Affairs, Rejoice Mabudafhasi, talking about a group of women who were keeping the ocean and the beaches clean in Durban.

"I thought to myself, we can do this. We have so many rivers here. I am not scared of challenges." She called the Deputy Minister herself, and that is how the Setsoto Women Empowerment Adopt-a-River Project came to be. The Caledon River, known as the Mohokare in Sesotho, journeys from Mont-Aux-Sources in the Drakensberg to the Orange River in the southern Free State. It marks the boundary between Lesotho and South Africa, and lends its grace to a fertile valley that was a source of conflict between the Boers and the Basotho people in the mid-19th Century. But to Thandazile, the river is life, and it pained her to see its waters strangled by waste and pollution.

With the backing of the Department of Water Affairs, she led a team of 30 women and six men on a cleanup to mark the start of the campaign. They wore blue overalls, red gloves, and yellow helmets, and they hefted dozens of bags of rubbish, plucked from the muddy banks. Because the riverine bushland can be dangerous, the department also provided the crew with first-aid kits and "tongs for handling snakes". Thandazile cannot speak for the men, but she knows that the women were not afraid, either of snakes or of getting their hands dirty.

She quotes a famous Sesotho saying: "*Mmangwana o tshwara thipa ka bohaleng*". The mother of a child holds the dagger on the sharp side.

"Women are the backbone of society," she says. "You teach a woman, you teach the nation." There are now more than 200 women who help to clean the river and its banks, in the small Free State towns of Ficksburg, Clocolan, Marquard, Senekal, and Fouriesburg. But she also thinks of her grandmother, who raised her and lifted her up, the MEC, Sisi Ntombela, who will always take her call and offer help and advice, and the women who sew and string beads and garden, to bring home money to feed their children.

"Women must help themselves," she says. In Sesotho, that translates as Itekeng Basadi Setsoto, which is the name of the sewing cooperative she formed at the centre, with four barely working machines. She has become adept at the art of writing funding proposals, and when she saw an invitation by the South African Broadcasting Corporation (SABC) Foundation on the internet, she applied for R100,000 to buy industrial-scale embroidery equipment. Her proposal was approved, but she had another request: "Please don't deposit this money. We will do a quotation and you will pay the supplier straight."

Managing a non-profit is a delicate business. You have to account for every cent of the money, and you have to make sure the money is spent on its express, intended purpose. The Japanese government made a donation of R1.3 million for the construction of a shelter at Itekeng. The contractor left before the job was finished. "I was so stressed, I didn't eat and I didn't sleep," says Thandazile. "I was asking myself, where will I get R1.3 million to finish this place? This is where God answered my prayer." A dozen workers from the township turned up. They said, don't worry, we will help you. They finished the job for free. But sometimes it is the other way round. People see Itekeng, and they think of it as a place that makes money. For that reason, the wrong reason, they want to be a part of it. "They don't know how hard it is to work here. They don't know how hard it is to communicate with funders, and how many proposals get rejected. They just see a millionaire. I have had to have meetings to explain this thing. I have had to say, it is not mine, it is for the community."

When staff at the centre take groceries for their own use, without asking, Thandazile has to say to them, this food doesn't belong to us, it belongs to the children. She has to say, this is not the meaning of Itekeng. To her it means inclusion, empowering, learning to make a difference. She sees herself as a social entrepreneur, not because she is building businesses, but because she is helping others to help others. Young people come to see her, Masechaba, the Mother of the Nation, and she tells them everything she has learned about starting an enterprise. The logistics, the funding, the administration, the big ideas, the small details, the management of people, expectations, and money. "I have created many things," she says. "Now I am motivating others. I give them advice and I walk with them on the road. But I tell them, you must know how to challenge the potholes. You must be fair, you must work hand in hand with your community. And all the time, you must put a smile on your face."

Her dream is that one day there will be a big factory at Itekeng, and the women who work there will have cars of their own to drive. There will be a bigger school with more classes, all the way from Grade 1 to 7. There will be a high school, called Itekeng High School for Disabled Children, and it will produce graduates who will go on to become nurses and doctors.

And here in her birthplace, her home, the centre of her calling, her legacy will be that she did what she could, what she had to, to turn a place of neglect into a place of hope and care.

Creating a Social, Political and Economic Marketplace for Change

In 1994 Peter Drucker floated the idea of a social not-for-profit, an organisation that had influence and impact across economic, social and political boundaries and that unwittingly strengthened both social cohesion and social capital (Wallace, 1999). It was an organisation that had an expanded impact, led by entrepreneurially minded people who were not content with the typical need–response approaches of the average civil society organisations (Wallace, 1999). Citing Ramsay, Dees, Drucker and others, Wallace (1999) comments that community leaders – or social entrepreneurs – recognised that they could not service or volunteer people out of poverty, and that a different approach was needed.

At first glance, Itekeng is a classic service-focused not-for-profit organisation, operating in the space of market and state failure, delivering a welfare service and relying on grant funding and goodwill to keep it going. But Itekeng is a great example of Drucker's social not-for-profit, as Thandazile's action in responding to the needs of deeply vulnerable, disabled children has had a catalytic effect on her community, engaging politicians, international funders and community members.

Thandazile has created a social, economic and political *marketplace* where people can engage and share value. Wallace (1999) describes the economic and social growth that occurs as a result of this community strengthening through redistributive goals.

The model opposite captures the impact of the social-purpose action that goes beyond the need–vision–action response that limits community development to a cause-and-effect cycle in which there is no systemic change. Because Mary's approach is anchored in the community, and she is so effective in building political, social and economic networks, the effect of her work is transformational. Mary strengthens the community infrastructure. She breaks out of the typical need–vision–action response, and has a socio-political impact on the community's economy (Drucker, 1994). Mary mobilises systemic change, regarded by Dees (2001) as an essential characteristic of a social entrepreneur.

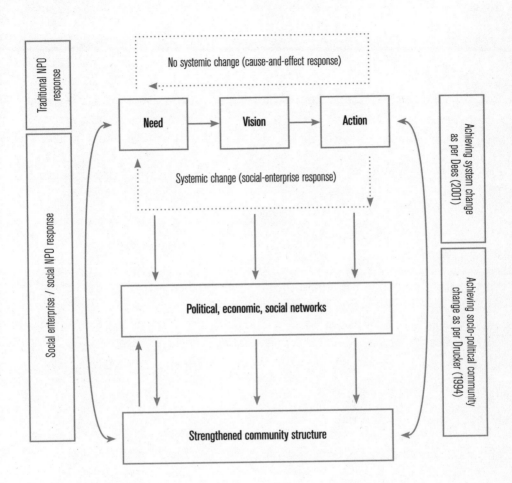

Social enterprise cycle of systemic change
Based on Wallace, 1999

MIND OF THE MAVERICK: PERSONALITY TRAITS OF SOCIAL ENTREPRENEURS

YUSUF RANDERA-REES

A New Revolution on Constitution Hill

Inspired by an epiphany while studying at Harvard and Oxford, Yusuf Randera-Rees came home to start an enterprise that is liberating potential and building a bold new generation of entrepreneurs

Hope rises above history on a hilltop in the heart of Johannesburg. From the ramparts, where prison guards used to patrol, you can look down on the gables and turrets of the Old Fort. You can wander into the eerily silent cells, where paint peels from the walls and sunlight casts shadows through the bars. The enemies of the state were confined here: the troublemakers and revolutionaries, the protesting students and striking workers. And with them, the everyday, ordinary lawbreakers: the brewers of illicit beer, the wanderers without passbooks after dark, the transgressors of the heavy line between black and white. The machinery of apartheid scooped them up, processed them, consigned them to their fate. But hope rises.

Step into the courtyard, and look up. On top of the brick stairwells of the old awaiting-trial blocks, towers of frosted glass soar into the sky, symbolising transparency and transformation. In the foyer of the Constitutional Court, staggered pillars evoke a forest, echoing the African tradition of justice convened in the shade of a tree. In a crucible on a stone step, a flickering flame represents the fragile wisp of democracy.

This is Constitution Hill. Everything on these grounds is a symbol, an abstract ideal given substance, shape, and form. So, too, with the Awethu Project, an incubator for entrepreneurs, housed in a modernist brick-and-iron building just across the knoll from the fort. "*Awethu*", which means "it is ours", is the rousing response to "*Amandla*", the call to power, that became the rallying cry of the liberation struggle in South Africa. Now the struggle is to liberate energy, ideas, and potential, to kindle ambition with opportunity, by giving aspirant entrepreneurs – the "previously unexplored", as one Awethu alumnus puts it – the guidance, mentorship, and resources to rise above their circumstances.

There is the airport-baggage handler who launched a thriving bread-delivery business in Alexandra township. There is the IT graduate who left

her job to supply home-made ginger beer, based on her mother's traditional recipe, for family functions and other social occasions. There is the high school dropout who pressed bricks by hand in an empty lot, and who now runs a brick-making plant employing more than 20 people. There is the rural villager who moved to Johannesburg to run township tours for overseas visitors, teaching them to sing and click their tongues in Xhosa.

For Yusuf Randera-Rees, these stories, and many more like them, are a validation, a proof of the concept that drew him back to South Africa, with a CV that could land him a high-flying job almost anywhere in the world. He is a Rhodes Scholar, a graduate of Oxford and Harvard, a derivatives trader who worked on Wall Street and in Zurich. But in 2009, he came home and founded the Awethu Project, with R60,000 of his own savings. He was 26 at the time, and his experience of the wider world had convinced him of one thing: that he was not as exceptional as the letters after his name made him out to be.

> "I knew there were people in South Africa who were more talented than me, smarter, more charismatic, better problem-solvers. Everything you would want in an entrepreneur, and they were not getting the opportunities I had been getting. That didn't make sense to me."

"I know my limitations," says Yusuf. "I knew there were people in South Africa who were more talented than me, smarter, more charismatic, better problem-solvers. Everything you would want in an entrepreneur, and they were not getting the opportunities I had been getting. That didn't make sense to me."

Today the Awethu Project manages over R160 million in government and corporate funding, and has kick-started the careers of more than 500 entrepreneurs. Candidates apply or are identified by talent scouts – the same process by which promising sports stars are discovered and nurtured – and the pick of the crop are put through an intensive mentoring and incubation programme: an Awethu Apprenticeship.

They are matched with pre-screened business opportunities, provided with infrastructure (office space, phones, internet-enabled computers), given a small startup budget and a monthly stipend, and the training and one-on-one support they need to craft a viable business plan and meet their profit targets. Those who succeed, after six months, become Awethu Entrepreneurs; those who do not, get a diploma and the dividends of their experience. But this is not, as Yusuf takes pains to point out, a charity or a corporate social investment initiative. It is a for-profit business partnership, with Awethu cutting equity deals in each business. The idea is to finesse and shape raw promise, and send it into the world on the wings of profit.

And yet, as soon as you walk into the headquarters of the Awethu Project, you get the sense that this is a political imperative too, that entrepreneurial development is the next frontier of the freedom struggle. In the reception area, there is a photograph of the most famous former prisoner of the Old Fort, Nelson Mandela, with his fist raised in salute to the slogan: "Let freedom reign". And on the wall of a workroom, where students tap away on laptops, are the larger-than-life images of two iconic role models, both named Steve: Biko, the founding father of Black Consciousness, and Jobs, the visionary genius of Apple.

Radical capitalism. Here at Awethu, it is not a culture shock or a paradox. It is chemistry in combustion. But to understand the mix, and what makes it work, we need to put Yusuf Randera-Rees himself in the spotlight for a while. He is lanky and engaging, a fast talker with a ready smile, his hair close-cropped to match his stubble. He is blue-eyed and fair of face, and over the years, he has grown accustomed to a discreet jolt from people who meet him for the first time and find that they have jumped to the wrong conclusion.

He illustrates the conundrum with a story from his schooldays. He was playing soccer at Old Edwardians in Johannesburg. "I was in a team huddle with all these white kids, and they saw a man coming over, and they said, 'Hey, look at this Indian guy, what does he want here?' And I said, 'No, that's my dad.'" Dr Fazel Randera. Born into a family of traders, he left Johannesburg as a teenager to study medicine in London. He was serving his residency when he met a Cambridge-educated doctor by the name of Helen Rees. They were from different worlds: she, from the green hills of Wales; he, from the war zone of apartheid. They fell in love. It was the early 1980s.

One day, Fazel saw footage, on a newscast, of a protest in Lenasia, a mostly Indian area of Johannesburg. Among the crowd, who were being baton-charged and teargassed by police, he recognised his young niece. He decided it was time to go back home. But the law would have prohibited Fazel and Helen from getting married in South Africa. And so, because of the Prohibition of Mixed Marriages Act and the Immorality Act, Yusuf was born in England, the first stage of a journey into identity that has left him free to think outside the tick-boxes of racial classification.

He remembers growing up in "this weird, mixed-race family", acutely conscious of being the only white-looking kid at family functions on his father's side.

"You stand out from everyone. You don't recognise anyone. Everyone knows you, but you don't know what the hell is going on. You are this little kid trying to understand culture. But it does force you not to box people. It leaves you freer, in a way, to do whatever you think."

He attended private, multiracial schools, Sacred Heart College and Crawford, allowing him to grow up as normally as possible in an abnormal society. But it was only when he got to Harvard, as an outstanding all-rounder, a sportsman with national colours and a former Junior Mayor of Johannesburg, that he began to feel the burden of his privilege. Daunted at first by his peers, the "kings of the universe", future leaders of nations and corporations, he had the epiphany that they were human after all, the carefully nurtured products of a simple formula for success.

> He was struck by the fact that 40 per cent of South Africans live on less than R800 a month, and in that group would be thousands of people who had never been given the chance to put their skills and talent to the test. The Previously Unexplored.

"You take world-class human talent, you invest world-class resources in that talent, and almost inevitably, you produce world-class businessmen, world-class leaders, and world-class scientists," says Yusuf. "I became very interested in the idea of whether South Africa is using our human talent, our potential, as well and as efficiently as they are at Harvard." The answer, from a distance, in the afterglow of the country's celebrated transition to democracy, was: sadly, no. The preamble of the Constitution of the Republic of South Africa lays the foundation for a society that will improve the quality of life and "free the potential" of each person. That hasn't turned out to be the case at all, says Yusuf.

"We cut the legs out from under the majority of the people, from the way we treat babies upwards. We write people off. We define them by their problems. That makes me angry, and I wanted to do something about it. That is why I started Awethu, to create a vehicle for people to realise their potential through business."

Yusuf wanted this vehicle to be fuelled by the high-octane impulse of entrepreneurial endeavour alone. The incentive, for the entrepreneur and the investor, would be the prospect of profit, profit, profit. The social impact would take care of itself. He was struck by the fact that 40 per cent of South Africans live on less than R800 a month, and in that group would be thousands of people who had never been given the chance to put their skills and talent to the test. The Previously Unexplored.

"You cannot argue that the reason they are poor is that they are not good enough," says Yusuf. Working with a Ghanaian-born friend, he came up with a model of financing and incubation to address what is known as the Missing Middle, the perplexing shortfall in the number of Small to Medium-sized Enterprises (SMEs) in the developing world. In high-income countries, SMEs account for 50 per cent of Gross Domestic Product (GDP) and 60 per cent of employment; in low-income countries, they account for less than half of that.

In 2009, Yusuf presented his proposal, for an Amandla Entrepreneurs Academy, at a business-plan competition in Oxford. There was a first prize of £20,000 up for grabs. "We got through to the finals," says Yusuf. "We were mentally spending the money. We did this sweet pitch with backing music. We thought we were so cool." They finished fourth.

The winning concept was a barrel-driven water-purification system for rural African women. But what really rankled, was a word of feedback from the judging panel. "They said our proposal was aspirational." To Yusuf, that was a put-down, a condescending dismissal of an idea that was designed to help ordinary people improve their lives meaningfully through entrepreneurship. But ideas are cheap. Deeds bring in the money.

One day, with his business partner, Ryan Pakter, a fellow Crawford and Harvard graduate, Yusuf drove into Alexandra township, one of the poorest areas of Johannesburg, just across the freeway from Sandton, one of the richest. They had a police escort, with blue lights flashing. "I hadn't spent much time in townships," says Yusuf. "What does a middle-class South African know about running a business in a township?" But he was willing to learn, and he had R60,000 of his own money invested in finding out if his hunch about talent was true.

They set up a table, shaded by beach umbrellas, with pamphlets and application forms and a handwritten sign, affixed to a fence with masking tape: "The Awethu Project". They were looking for young South Africans, 22 to 35, no experience necessary, who had "never had access to systematic opportunity". More than 1000 wannabe entrepreneurs applied. Later, they screened the applicants, using cognitive tests aimed at identifying entrepreneurial abilities. The psychometrist called Yusuf on the first day of testing and said, I have good news and I have bad news. "Give me the good news," said Yusuf.

"'Man,' he said to me, 'your smartest guy is as smart as anyone in the world.' So I said, 'That is amazing, what is the bad news?' And he said, 'I think it is a white Afrikaans guy. His name is Chris Pienaar.' I said, 'There is no chance.'" It turned out that Chris, just like Yusuf, had mixed ancestry. He owed his Afrikaans surname to his grandfather. At the time, Chris, a bright student who had routinely scored 100 per cent for maths at school, was selling beer from his backyard in Alex. After his incubation at Awethu, he launched a food-delivery service called Straight to Your Door. For Yusuf, Chris is a working model of the Awethu vision: breaking the glass ceiling from informal to formal business.

Three of the original selection of six Awethu Entrepreneurs went from making R3,000 a month to R15,000 a month after graduating. But Awethu itself needed an injection of cash to survive, and the big windfall came with the 2011 launch of the Treasury's Jobs Fund, a R9-billion government initiative to co-finance innovative projects capable of creating sustainable jobs. Awethu was given an initial grant of R20 million.

"I remember sitting on the couch with my mom and telling her, and she just went, Sho! What do you do with R20 million? Up to that point, we had spent a combined total of R1.5 million. We quickly became an institution." In a few months, Awethu went from two employees to 50 employees, and from three entrepreneurs to 500 entrepreneurs, out of a total of 30,000 applicants.

For some entrepreneurs, the trajectory was so rapid that it overtook their commitment to share their profits with Awethu. "There was a plumber who was making R1,000," says Yusuf, "and we helped him get municipal contracts for R1 million a month. Then he didn't want to answer the phone." On a micro scale, the incentives were all wrong. You under-report profits, because you don't want to share. You don't report jobs, because jobs are an indicator of profit. "So we said, okay, fine, we'll put a freeze on fees. And suddenly, everything went through the roof. The social outcome was better when we stopped trying to make money."

For Yusuf, this is the key to making Awethu work. Focus on creating entrepreneurs who make money and create jobs. He believes Awethu's entrepreneurs can make as much money, an average of R20 million in a 20-year career, as graduates of Harvard Business School.

"Don't get paid in people slapping you on the back," he says. "People will tell you that you are doing great things, well done. But what is the net benefit to anybody? Zero. I think that is a danger for talented social entrepreneurs. Good feeling is cheap. People give it away."

So he works, and he works hard. An average of 70 to 100 hours a week. He has an old yellow Volvo, but he takes an Uber wherever he goes, because it gives him time and space to get things done. He has learned some key lessons since he came home, with his Harvard and Oxford degrees, in 2009. One is that hard work isn't enough to build a business. Nor is talent, and nor is a good idea.

"Just because someone has investable talent," he says, "doesn't make their business investable." One of the primary innovations at Awethu was to "decouple the horse from the jockey", the entrepreneur from the idea.

"Everybody else will tell you that the entrepreneur comes up with the idea, and that is how an investment fund works. There is this magic thing where an entrepreneur loves their idea, they are passionate about it, and they run their business and it is amazing. But there are not enough entrepreneurs with ideas, especially in the informal sector. So what we do is create a pipeline of ideas, people and capital, and bring them together to produce successful businesses."

One example: someone emails Yusuf to say, we're looking for a black, female-owned events-management company, do you have one? No. So come up with one. Find the right person, invest training and money, and make it happen. Because development funds are naturally risk averse, Awethu also raises its own capital, through the Small Enterprise Finance Agency, an SME arm of the Industrial Development Corporation (IDC). This allows Awethu to invest up to R2.5 million in a business proposal. On a typical day, Yusuf will have up to 30 proposals on his table.

"It's an exciting position to be in, having to understand so many different ideas and people every day," he says. It reminds him of a sport he did at Oxford: modern pentathlon. In one day, you fence in a round-robin contest, you swim 200 metres freestyle, you run cross-country for 3.2 kilometres, you ride a horse over 12 to 15 obstacles, and you shoot at a stationary target from a distance of 10 metres.

Yusuf wants Awethu to be a R1-billion enterprise by 2020, creating 50 businesses a month, with a model that can easily be replicated across Africa. He wants to see a generation of emerging business leaders who can live up to that line in the preamble to the Constitution: to free the potential of every person.

"To be good at modern pentathlon, you have to be good at a variety of skills and disciplines. It's similar to Awethu in that here you have to quickly understand dozens of business models and the entrepreneurs trying to make them happen."

The rules of the game are changing. Yusuf tells the story of Lesika Matlou, one of the first entrepreneurs to go through the Awethu programme.

"He comes from a mining community. Everyone he knows became a miner. His dad has been a blaster for 30 years. When he came here, his dad told him this is not what a man does. A man goes to the mines."

A few years later, Lesika appeared on a TV ad for Awethu. He was running a tour company called Ek Sê Tours. He was turning over R1 million a year, and employing eight people. His dad sent his brother to live with him, to learn how to be an entrepreneur.

"That is a perfect little microcosm of how you change the way things are," says Yusuf. "I think South Africa is ripe for change, and I feel these guys are perfectly positioned to create that change."

Yusuf wants Awethu to be a R1-billion enterprise by 2020, creating 50 businesses a month, with a model that can easily be replicated across Africa. He wants to see a generation of emerging business leaders who can live up to that line in the preamble to the Constitution: to free the potential of every person.

Here on Constitution Hill, after you have finished your wanderings, you will find a small al fresco café and bar, with a plywood deck and sail-like awnings, called The Hill. The manager is a tall, soft-spoken ex-Zimbabwean named Vincent Chipendo, who worked in the kitchen of a steakhouse before he applied for a mentorship at the Awethu Project.

Making sure everyone at the tables is happy, he pauses to tend his herb and vegetable garden, growing healthily on a sill opposite the Old Fort. One day, perhaps, Vincent will own this place on the hill. Hard work, courage, and an investment in your potential, are all it takes to bring your hopes to harvest.

ACCESS TO COURTS

You have the right to resolve your legal disputes in a court or another impartial tribunal.

RESPONSIBILITIES

All citizens are equally subject to the duties and responsibilities of citizenship.

ARRESTED, DETAINED & ACCUSED PERSONS

en arrested for allegedly committed offence, you have the right to remain nt, to be brought before a court within hours and the right to legal resentation.

CULTURAL, RELIGIOUS & LINGUISTIC COMMUNITIES

You have the right to form, join and maintain cultural, linguistic and religious grouping of your own choice.

Uncoupling the Entrepreneur from the Idea

Drakopoulou Dodd and Anderson (2007) write of the mythical entrepreneurial hero, who society has idolised, revelling in their individual passion, drive, resilience and maverick idea that ultimately catalyses change. But they argue that it is not these individual attributes that drive the entrepreneur, but rather their social context that not only enables them to achieve change, but fuels it – "entrepreneurs draw from and give back to the social" (Drakopoulou Dodd & Anderson, 2007, p. 342).

Yusuf Randera-Rees is typical of this approach to entrepreneurship. He is deeply connected to societal realities and consequently so is his approach to entrepreneurship. He does this first by uncoupling the entrepreneur and the idea, instantly transforming the entrepreneur from what Johannisson (1998) describes as the individual adventurously projecting their vision and making it happen. Instead, Awethu focuses on *networking* the entrepreneur, connecting them to support structures and the partners they need to make the idea work. Drakopoulou Dodd and Anderson (2007) describe this approach as the Networked Entrepreneur; entrepreneurs who succeed because they have the support of diverse teams, and build relationships and interactions that enable them to navigate both the opportunity and constraint systems of their context. The Networked Entrepreneur remains "at the centre of the entrepreneurial stage" (Drakopoulou Dodd & Anderson, 2007, p. 342), supported by their social context that helps drive, produce and use their product – and consequently their success.

This theory is supported by Corner and Ho (2010) who find that two characteristics that distinguish social entrepreneurs from their for-profit counterparts is, firstly, their collective approach: because the ultimate goal is social-value creation, they are naturally collaborative, recognising that they cannot achieve this in isolation. Secondly, their contextual knowledge and understanding drives the entrepreneurial idea and therefore is inherent to the make-up of the social entrepreneur.

The model shows how Awethu networks their entrepreneurs, connecting them with their ideas, and supporting them. It also illustrates Yusuf's approach to social entrepreneurship. He uses the social context as the foundation for being a networked entrepreneur. In this way, Yusuf and Awethu's entrepreneurs are better able to navigate the unique opportunities and constraints inherent to social entrepreneurship.

Able to navigate both systems of constraint and opportunity

Build relationships

Support of diverse teams

| Entrepreneur | Idea |

Connected

Systems of support

The networked entrepreneur

Yusuf's approach

Awethu's approach

| Informs need | Requires collaborative entrepreneurship | Social context is market |

Social context

"Entrepreneurs draw from and give back to the social" – Yusuf and Awethu as the networked entrepreneur

Based on Drakopoulou Dodd and Anderson, 2007

GARTH JAPHET

THE HEART AND SOUL OF DR GARTH JAPHET

Driven by his childhood dream of becoming a doctor, he turned primary healthcare into primetime entertainment, and positive values into a platform for building a better society

The doctor steered his Land Rover through the thick red mud, headlights illuminating the torrents of rain that had burst the banks of the river. In the dark of night, the call had come, a desperate, breathless cry for help from the nurse at the clinic. His vehicle swayed, like a ship at sea, as it sought a grip amidst the surging waters. He was on his way to save a life, and in so doing, bring another life into the world. The engine cut with a splutter, and he waded the last few metres, black bag in hand, towards the ghostly flicker of the lamp in the room. The patient looked up, eyes too tired to focus. She was hardly out of childhood herself. The doctor put on his stethoscope and listened to the soft, low beating of the unborn baby's heart. He had come just in time. Get ready, nurse, he said. We're going to have to do an emergency caesarean.

In a suburban home in Johannesburg, a boy named Garth Japhet turned the page of his bedtime storybook, enthralled. In *Jungle Doctor*, a series of dramatic tales by Paul White, an Australian missionary and evangelist who had worked as a rural doctor in East Africa, he had found a calling and a hero. Garth wanted to be a doctor too, saving lives, fighting lions, hacking his way through the jungle, dropping packs of antibiotics into villages from his twin-prop plane. There were just two small things standing in his way. One, he fainted at the sight of blood. Two, his average mark in matric, maths and science included, was a C.

But there is value in a childhood dream, and value in pursuing it, even when the career-guidance counsellor looks down at you and says, "It would be wise not to choose medicine." Wisely, he didn't listen. Through sheer grit and determination, Garth graduated from medical school, and yes, when he delivered his first baby, he fell flat in a faint on the floor. Happily, the baby was fine, and the doctor picked himself up, dusted himself off, and went on to revive his career as a primary care physician. He worked in rural clinics, just like his childhood hero, but looking back, he says he would have liked to

specialise. "If I was more technically proficient," says Garth, "I would love to have done ophthalmology. It's such an amazing discipline. You make such a difference to people. They walk in there with cataracts, and they come out and they can see. It's very immediate. It's very practical."

And yet, even though he no longer practises as a clinician, he too has opened eyes, and along with them, hearts and minds. Today he is Dr Garth Japhet, social entrepreneur, founder of the healthcare drama series, Soul City, and the positive-values campaign, Heartlines. His medicine of choice, his prescription for a better way of living your life, is… stories. Find them, explore them, craft them, tell them, share them, listen to them, interpret them, illuminate them. Above all, learn from them, because this is the real wonder of stories: that they dress enlightenment in the costumes of character and emotion, to show us who we are and what we can aspire to be. But if there is one thing Garth learned from the Jungle Doctor, it is that you have to weather the storm, and find your own way to cast a light in people's lives.

> Above all, learn from them, because this is the real wonder of stories: that they dress enlightenment in the costumes of character and emotion, to show us who we are and what we can aspire to be.

First came Soul City, the pioneering public-health organisation behind the radio and television drama series that has been running for as long as South Africa's democracy. Launched in 1994, as a platform for turning primary healthcare messages into primetime entertainment, the series has inspired behavioural change, influenced national policy, and blurred the boundary between fiction and everyday life. Proof of Soul City's foothold in the popular imagination is that there are at least 11 informal settlements in South Africa that have named themselves after the show. In the hard-hitting, emotionally charged style of a soap opera, the series plots itself around the very real issues that affect community life, among them HIV/Aids, domestic violence, alcohol abuse, teenage pregnancy, poverty, and unemployment.

Soul City opens a window on people's lives, and in so doing, through the magic of storytelling, the window becomes a mirror. "Know thyself," as the ancient Delphic maxim puts it. Soul City is not just an institution, it's an institute, a non-profit, non-governmental organisation funded by private companies, international aid donors, and the South African Departments of Health and Social Development. Soul City employs a team of more than 200, reaching millions across Africa through the broadcast series and spinoffs, such as Soul Buddyz, aimed at children and teenagers, Rise, aimed at young women, and *Kwanda* ("To grow"), a reality TV show that encourages people to work together to improve their lives and communities. Soul City is a bustling multimedia metropolis of social enterprise, but for Garth, it became a metropolis with walls, and beyond them he could see other possibilities, other communities, other missions and callings.

"Soul City has got equal brand recognition with Coca-Cola amongst black people," says Garth, "but white people hardly know about it. My sense is that a lot of the big issues we face are not just black issues. There are issues that need to be embraced by the entire population, particularly those with means." So in 2008, he left Soul City, to follow his heart and tell a bigger story of who we are and what we aspire to be. A story of the ties that bind us, the values we share, the lines that connect our higher ideals to the everyday lives we live on the ground. The lines of the human heart.

Heartlines, which spreads its message of positive values and good citizenship through TV, cinema, outreach programmes and storytelling campaigns, is an NPO, funded by commercial and non-commercial donors, including banks, technology companies, and international foundations. But it works in tandem with a for-profit enterprise called Forgood, a web-based platform for mobilising and connecting volunteers with causes they wish to support. "Heartlines is an NPO and it doesn't make any profit," explains Garth. And then, with a shrug: "Forgood is a for-profit, and it doesn't make any profit either." Well, at least, not yet. Garth's premise with Forgood was to replicate the spirit and reach of Soul City on the internet. But he underestimated the costs and challenges of building a digital platform, and getting a team of outsourced web developers to work together with his team of "bleeding hearts". It was a nightmare initially, he says, "but thankfully it is now fully back on track". Forgood's business model is based on licensing to corporates, explains Garth. "It tracks, monitors, and reports on activity. It enables corporates to scale up and do real-time reporting on their community engagement programmes."

For the social entrepreneur, schooled in the discipline of working for the greater good, running an enterprise with a profit motive calls for a major shift in thought and action. But perhaps the guiding principle lies in the title of the most ambitious Heartlines project to date: *Nothing for Mahala*. This is a commercial movie, released in 2013, about a reckless young spendthrift who lives a fast and flashy life. Too fast. Sentenced to community service for a traffic violation, he meets his polar opposite, a grumpy old man who threw away his own money and ruined his relationships. Now, trapped in an old-age home, he is bristling with resentment and regret. In each other, the young man and the old man see a mirror and a shot at redemption. The message, veiled in knockabout comedy, is that money is only worth something if it adds value to life, because the true currency of happiness is human connection. "Mahala" is slang for, well, nothing. You get nothing for nothing in this world, but hard, honest toil can be a reward on its own. A value right up there with kindness, compassion, courage, integrity, perseverance, and respect.

The question is, do we need a movie to tell us these things? Do we need TV flightings, print and radio campaigns, storybooks for children, a music CD with an all-star cast? Are values not innate, handed down through the generations, woven into the ethos of family and faith, and the teachings of the education system? Should we not know values off by heart? Garth is a self-confessed romantic, a Christian, an idealist. But he is a realist too: "While we may aspire to live good values," he says, "we often do the things that we do not want to do." Stories, well-told, can help us tell the difference and show us the better way, "to live our higher selves", as Garth says. The clinician learns that you don't just treat the illness and strive to cure the disease. You try to prevent it from happening in the first place. Heartlines launched in 2006, with a massive multimedia blitz, funded by First National Bank, called "8 Weeks. 8 Values. 1 National Conversation". The crux of it was a series of eight films, screened on all three channels by the national broadcaster, SABC. Each film dramatised a positive value, through ordinary people struggling to put it into practice: Acceptance; Responsibility; Forgiveness; Perseverance; Self-Control; Honesty; Compassion; and Second Chances. The goal was to get people talking, arguing, debating, opening up, questioning their own value systems, sharing their own stories, starting conversations through the catharsis of testimony. Heartlines is a campaign of revival, a return to basics, a "Reconstruction and Development Programme of the heart" as Garth puts it. Once again, it is dressed in the cloth of popular entertainment, communicated through the secular evangelism of social media.

Garth doesn't shy away from the fundament of faith that anchors Heartlines, which "acknowledges God as the authority of all good values". Rather, he points out that faith is "South Africa's biggest social network", with 65 per cent of the population attending a faith-based institution at least once a month. "The reality is that if people lived what they believed," says Garth, "we would transform everything. But the values we promote are embraced by people of no faith as well."

Leaving Soul City, with its emphasis on the corporeal, and its abundant resources for telling and sharing stories, was an act of faith in itself. In November 2013, when Heartlines was struggling to raise funding for new projects, Garth called in his team, about a dozen-strong, and said, "Guys, we're out of money come end of February." He offered them a severance package and leads for new jobs. "And not one person left," says Garth. "They all stayed. For me, that was proof enough that they believe in the mission of the organisation, and that living positive values begins at home."

Sitting in the office of Heartlines in Dunkeld, Johannesburg, just a door away from his old office at Soul City, Garth is personable, expansive, earnest about his work, but with a dry sense of humour that plays most often on his own perceived flaws and insecurities. To begin with, he confesses, he was a bit of a problem child, not in the sense of misbehaviour, but in the sense of a broader malaise, a pervasive anxiety that he now diagnoses as SHS. "Stuffed-Head Syndrome," he explains. "That's when your head is stuffed, basically. I was quite a disturbed kid. Highly anxious; a psychologist's dream. I had a big sense of failure and insecurity. I think that's where it comes from, this burning ambition to succeed, to prove people wrong."

He was the youngest by far of four siblings, and he spent much of his time alone, lost in books, his imagination running wild and free. He drifted from school to school – "I even dropped out of nursery school," he says – before landing up in a private cram-college, the last refuge of the academically disinclined. He was allowed to skip a year, which was good for his self-esteem, but not for his marks. From his father, a lawyer and businessman who was active in opposition politics, he absorbed a sense of social justice, a value that only sharpened his zeal for becoming a doctor. He volunteered at hospitals, which is where he discovered his queasiness at the sight of blood, and he completed his A levels in England, allowing him to scrape into medical school on the basis of "other criteria".

> He was a bit of a problem child, not in the sense of misbehaviour, but in the sense of a broader malaise, a pervasive anxiety that he now diagnoses as SHS. "Stuffed-Head Syndrome," he explains.

But the real world of medicine, he soon found out, was different to the romanticised world of Jungle Doctor. He hated the early years of med school, but as a more senior undergrad once told him, "don't worry, you'll get over it". Meaning, you'll conquer your foolish idealism and go on to be a doctor, making a good living.

Then, in 1990, as the country laboured painfully from apartheid into democracy, Garth was stationed at a rural clinic in Pietermaritzburg, KwaZulu-Natal, at the peak of internecine violence between supporters of the African National Congress (ANC) and the Inkatha Freedom Party (IFP). "It was what they called the Seven-Day War," says Garth. "I ended up being a doctor responsible for 15,000 refugees overnight." Surrounded by pain and trauma, escorted by soldiers with guns, he had the first of what he calls his many existential crises, a questioning of his worth and purpose that continued when he moved to Johannesburg to run a paediatric unit at Alexandra Clinic. Here, in a poverty-stricken, run-down township just across the freeway from the wealthy suburb of Sandton, he began to realise that being a doctor can mean more than just preventing and treating disease. It can also be a form of teaching, of telling stories to promote good health. Garth went to see Aggrey Klaaste, Editor of *The Sowetan*, famous for his nation-building initiative, through which he hoped to inspire South Africans to repair the damage caused by apartheid. "Because I was a doctor, I was able to walk right into his office," jokes Garth.

At the time, *The Sowetan* was the biggest-circulation daily newspaper in Johannesburg. "I said, I'd like to write for you. And to his credit, he said, fine." Garth's weekly column, also syndicated in *The Star*, was called "The Healthy Nation". He used drama and analogy to communicate the basics of primary health and wellness. "I would use stories to try and get the concepts across. A guy pulls into a petrol station, and by mistake, he gets his car tyres pumped up too much. On the highway, he gets a blowout and he dies. It's the same with your body. Your blood vessels are like car tyres. If the pressure gets too high, they'll have a blowout."

The column had an avid following, but Garth still felt he was "going nowhere in a hurry": what about people who didn't read the papers? He thought about TV or radio, maybe a gameshow, using his experiences at the clinic as a basis for telling stories to as big an audience as possible. He had found his purpose. Now all he had to do was find out what it was worth.

Garth may be harsh about what he sees as his weaknesses, but he admits he has two redeeming qualities. Perseverance, and optimism. Add to that, chutzpah: the gall to put forward a crazy proposition. He managed to persuade his media partner – *The Sowetan* – to pay the clinic his salary for three months, allowing them to hire a locum to take his place, while he took a sabbatical to raise funding and develop a pilot for the TV soap opera that would become *Soul City*. The doctor had become the storyteller. The storyteller would become the social entrepreneur.

Today, as he grapples with the value of values, trying to find a way to link them to the lines of the heart, he has to grapple too with where the money is coming from. "What is exciting," says Garth, "is that beyond traditional donors, a new breed of investor is emerging. They are interested in investing if there is a social return, even if the financial return is much lower. This is giving rise to business models where people are aiming to do good, as well as to do well." The big question is, can you quantify doing good? Can you measure the social return on investment? Yes, says Garth, down to the finest percentage. In an independent evaluation report of the impact of the seventh series of *Soul City* on a nationally representative sample of South Africans, for instance, the series was directly credited with raising condom usage by up to 21 per cent. And 18 per cent of people exposed to *Soul City* reported that they had taken part in community activities to support people with HIV/Aids, double the amount in a control group. On the Heartlines side, Garth says more than 12 million people have been reached by the films, stories, and resources. But that's just a start.

"I'm probably too dumb to know when I'm beaten," says Garth. But faith is a kind of defiance too, and Garth has enough of it to believe in himself. "I think a lot of people give up too easily," he says. "It's amazing how many times I have been just about to give up, and I carry on, and things turn around. What keeps me going are the people I work with. I think we've got a happy place here." He's come to terms with the fact that the world, in itself, can't be saved, and that you may never, in the words of Gandhi, get to be the change you want to see. He is happy enough that the difference he is making now could help to build a better world for future generations. And more than anything, he has learned that if you put your heart and soul into it, you can be lucky enough to make your childhood dream come true. Looking back now, he realises that it wasn't that he wanted to be a doctor in the jungle. What he really wanted to do was tell stories to help heal the world.

The DIY Social Entrepreneur

*B*ricolage is French for "Do It Yourself", a term that has gained traction in the entrepreneurship field, meaning "making do with what is at hand" (Di Domenico, Haugh & Tracey, 2010, p. 684). Garth can be considered a serial social entrepreneur, someone who is constantly looking for new ways to shift systems, setting up organisations to achieve change with a canny ability to see and therefore use what is at hand. His ideas are shaped by the end purpose he wants to achieve, and that purpose is shaped by the resources available (Di Domenico et al., 2010). He is a social-entrepreneur bricoleur.

Di Domenico, Haugh and Tracey (2010) describe the qualities of the social-entrepreneur bricoleur as always making do, refusing to be constrained by the limitations of their environment, improvising, creating social value and engaging their stakeholders. "Making do" is creating something from nothing; using discarded, unwanted or hidden resources for new purposes in ways that others haven't thought of. Garth made do by using the potential of mass media to communicate public-health messages in an entertaining way.

A Deep Desire to Spark Social Change

Social-entrepreneur bricoleurs refuse to be constrained by the inherently constrained systems they choose to operate in. They "consciously and consistently" (p. 692) develop solutions that subvert the difficulties of their environments in order to create social value (Di Domenico et al., 2010). They are excellent improvisers, creative problem-solvers who change course when necessary (Di Domenico et al., 2010). Garth is constantly improvising, working around resource limitations by setting up for- and not-for-profit business models; striving for new ways to deliver social value through new ventures.

Garth is motivated by social-value creation and stakeholder participation. Soul City grew into a complex NPO, with multiple layers of community involvement, which informed the content of the TV and radio programmes – creating social value. Garth instinctively recognised that you can't have social-value creation without stakeholder participation, and continued this approach in the community work of Heartlines and in the networking of Forgood.

The model shows how Garth is the quintessential social-entrepreneur bricoleur: his DIY toolkit navigates constraints, consciously and consistently developing solutions by improvising, problem-solving, and involving others to achieve social value.

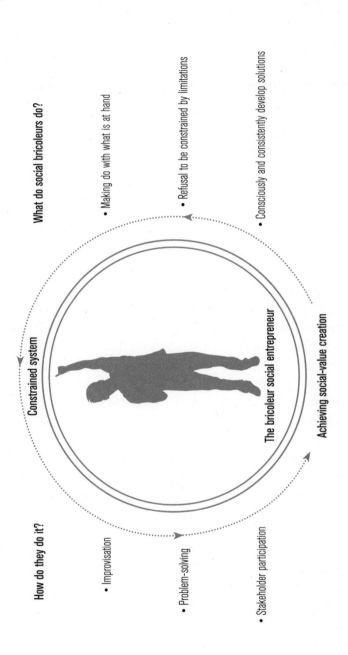

What do social bricoleurs do?

- Making do with what is at hand
- Refusal to be constrained by limitations
- Consciously and consistently develop solutions

Constrained system

The bricoleur social entrepreneur

Achieving social-value creation

How do they do it?

- Improvisation
- Problem-solving
- Stakeholder participation

The bricoleur social entrepreneur – a constant cycle of "making do"

Based on Di Domenico et al., 2010

SHARANJEET SHAN

THE MEANING OF LOVE IS MATHEMATICS

Banished from her home in Punjab, India, for the transgression of falling in love, Sharanjeet Shan sought refuge in the joy of mathematics and teaching, finding her life's mission in helping young South Africans from disadvantaged communities see the power and wonder of maths and science

Early one weekday morning, a football flies through the air in a primary school classroom somewhere in Johannesburg. To stand in its path is to be put on the spot, like a goalkeeper facing a penalty. "Three times five?" asks the teacher, picking a boy from the semicircle in front of the chalkboard. He catches the ball with both hands. "Fifteen!" And he throws it back. "Two times ten?" A girl catches the ball. "Twenty!" She throws it back. The game speeds up, a calculated chain of call and response that puts quick thinking and reflexes to the test. "Three times four?" This time, the catcher hesitates, holding on to the ball for a fraction too long. "Who can help her?" The hands shoot up, fingers clicking. "Twelve!" a learner says, and she arcs the ball back with a smile.

In another classroom, a hand drives a string of digits and symbols, stacking them row upon row on a whiteboard, until the flourish of an equals sign heralds the triumphant conclusion. The elements fall into place, like the click of a key turning in a lock. The universe is made of mathematics. Everywhere you look, there are patterns and shapes and sequences, overlapping, interconnecting, alive with energy and meaning. The spiral of a galaxy is echoed in the swirl of a shell; the fire at the heart of a distant star finds its mirror in a sunflower's flare. The infinite and the infinitesimal are bound as one, brought together by order born from chaos.

In the path of a theorem chalked on a board, darkness gives way to light, ignorance to understanding, problem to solution. The beauty of pure logic defines the quantum of life. We count, therefore we are. A teacher is a messenger sent by the gods to show us how to unravel the secrets one by one.

But when Sharanjeet Shan arrived from England, at the dawn of South Africa's democracy in 1994, she was surprised to learn that the teachers needed teaching more than the learners. She was a maths and science

teacher with a Masters in Social Sciences, an adviser and inspector with the Sandwell Education Authority in West Midlands, England, and a youth leader and community activist, dedicated to fighting racism in the classroom.

She had been headhunted, after a chance meeting with a South African delegation at an education conference in Québec, Canada, to take charge of a non-profit institution called Maths Centre, which at the time was a small "outreach project" operating in Gauteng and Mpumalanga. She wasn't quite sure what that would mean in practice, but she was immediately disheartened when she found out. "It was bad," she says. "Really, really bad. There were eight or nine trainers who themselves had not studied mathematics, but they were going into schools advising on mathematics. It was like the blind leading the blind. And I was very incensed and offended by that."

On the verge of turning 50, she had been drawn into a change of place and pace, not just by the challenge of starting afresh, but by the chance to walk in the footsteps of two of her greatest role models. Mahatma Gandhi, the lawyer who was stirred into a campaign of passive resistance against the might of the British Empire during his political awakening in South Africa, and Stephen Bantu Biko, the martyred icon of the Black Consciousness Movement. Instead, she found herself talking to government official after government official, about the urgent need to address the shortcomings in maths and science education.

"Why do your children not succeed?" she would ask. "You've got teachers. You've got a Department of Education. Surely, you have policies and practices that can be disseminated. And there are statutory instruments and, using all of those, you can begin to gain advantages for black African children." But that was precisely why she had been called. Because she asked uncomfortable questions. Because she challenged conventional wisdoms. Because she refused to accept convenient excuses or the dereliction of promise and potential. And so, because she had travelled a long way, and because Gandhi and Biko would not have turned back, she stepped into her tenure as Executive Director of the Maths Centre, and she began to do her job, which, at first, was to open people's eyes. Not everyone liked what they saw.

There were two petitions filed against her in the early years of her tenure, calling for the board to send her back to England. "They said that my style is very harsh and difficult and that I have no Struggle credentials," says Sharanjeet. "I expect people to have a lot of discipline. I expect people to achieve a lot." She had imposed a strict regime of training on the trainers, who would go on to train other trainers in poorly resourced, underperforming primary and high schools across the country. "It was heartbreaking," she says of the response.

"How did I come out of it? How do I normally come out from any crisis? I am a pretty hardcore Sufi. Sufism, as you know, is a branch of Islam where love is understood in its real essence amongst human beings."

Love and discipline. The formula worked. Today, Maths Centre is a model of what can be achieved through rigorous, radical devotion to a cause, and an uncompromising, scientific approach to best practice in education. The centre, now nationwide, develops and runs maths and science programmes for learners from Grade R to matric, and trains teachers. While Sharanjeet was recruited for her skills as an educator and manager, she has proved herself to be a social entrepreneur by transforming Maths Centre into a sustainable organisation with multiple streams of revenue.

"Social entrepreneurs are disruptors of a kind, big-time dreamers," says Sharanjeet, who won a Schwab Foundation Social Entrepreneur of the Year Award in 2015. "Their life story is woven into their dream. Even when there may be deep tears in the fabric of their journey, the dreamers believe in their cause to a level of madness."

As a non-profit institution, Maths Centre is funded largely by corporate sponsorships and projects, which contribute about 85 per cent of the running costs. The rest comes from the direct selling of materials and training.

In 2014, on a budget of R48 million, the centre had more than 174,000 learners and 4,200 educators, supporting 520 schools across the country. The big dividend was the matric pass rate: more than 81 per cent of Maths Centre Grade 12s passed maths at the required level for tertiary education, and more than 85 per cent made the grade in physical science. Compare this with a figure Sharanjeet quotes as evidence of an education system where 12 years of schooling simply don't add up: of more than a million learners who started school in 2003, only 30,287 would emerge with a pass in matric maths in 2014. In percentage terms, that's…well, you're probably not going to get the answer from the remaining 970,000 or so. For Sharanjeet, this is a national tragedy, a symptom of a learning space which is "nothing but a cauldron of misery, mistrust, boredom, confusion and conflict". Against this background, Maths Centre is a beacon of a better approach, with quantifiably positive outcomes, and few would deny that its success is at least in part a tribute to the defiant, unquenchable spirit of its Executive Director.

> Love and discipline. The formula worked. Today, Maths Centre is a model of what can be achieved through rigorous, radical devotion to a cause, and an uncompromising, scientific approach to best practice in education.

Sharanjeet – whose name means "one who attains the shelter of the guru, wins" – was a student herself when she was banished to England from her birthplace in the Punjab region of India. Her offence, against culture, tradition, and honour, was that she had fallen in love – the most ancient and natural of all human equations – but she had fallen on the wrong side of the divide. She was 19, in the final year of her medical degree, and she intended to marry a doctor, who was a Muslim. She reasoned that her father, a Sikh army officer – "his job was to shoot down planes" – would be proud enough of his gifted child to make an allowance for her headstrong indiscretion. He was not. "All hell broke loose," she says.

She is a teacher, and she has learned that any problem, any conundrum, can be solved if you break it down to its core components, a series of steps that you follow until they dance you into the light.

Far from the shelter of a benevolent guru, she was confined by her father to a small, lightless room. He would let her out only to be beaten on her hands and knees, and fed a wild bloom that made her hallucinate. For nine months, this was her fate, and then she was declared null and cast into the void. Her father married her by arrangement to a Hindu man, a cost accountant, and they went to live in the quiet green countryside in England. "Unfortunately," she says, "the husband was equally abusive." Her father had declared an honour killing – "as far as we are concerned, she is dead" – and in this strange land of her limbo and resurrection, she brought up two boys, her dream of being a doctor deferred, as her husband took ill and slowly faded, like a ghost.

Sharanjeet began to see her misfortune as a gift, because it forced her to recalibrate her life, and to realise that her calling was not to heal, but to teach. "My father's abuse of me was the greatest gift," she says. "My husband's abuse of me was the greatest gift. When you think of things in that way, then there can be a bigger lesson." She had lost all contact with her family in the Punjab, but the words of her great aunt lingered like a mantra. "Problems that will defeat me, destiny has not yet designed."

In her office at the headquarters of Maths Centre in Braamfontein, Johannesburg, against the backdrop of a painting of a school of fish evolving into a flock of birds, Sharanjeet laughs. "It sounds better," she says, "in the original Punjabi." She wears a bright yellow dress, Punjabi-style, dotted with circles and whorls, a fulsome necklace of glass beads, African-style, sapphire earrings, and a shock of silver hair. She has just turned 70, and she is illuminated by a playful optimism, a zest for finding and sharing the wonder in life. She has been blessed with the greatest gift: the gift of being able to give others the gift of learning.

She is a teacher, and she has learned that any problem, any conundrum, can be solved if you break it down to its core components, a series of steps that you follow until they dance you into the light. But the great problem, here in her adoptive motherland, is that too many people do not know the steps. The maths dances around and without them, drifting into a blur. You can hear the music, but it sounds like noise. Then along comes the teacher, and slowly, she tunes you in. It is not an easy task, admits Sharanjeet.

Every year, when the results come out, she feels weighed down by the burden, the lag between our aspirations and our performance as a nation. The Trends in International Mathematics and Science Study, which is conducted every four years across the globe, ranks South Africa 148th out of 148 countries for the quality of its maths and science education. You could try to see the bright side in that, and argue that it is at least a good base for improvement. But an economy without a superstructure of maths and science is like a castle made of sand, waiting for the tide to rush in. You can't build a bridge without maths. You can't fly a plane without maths. You can't run a bank without maths. You can't innovate, invent, compete and grow without a corps of scientists, mathematicians, engineers and technologists to fly the flag.

"Raise your hand if you loved maths at school." That's what Sharanjeet will say when she starts a talk to an audience of grown-ups. "I am lucky to have five per cent of the audience respond positively," she says. Then she will tell them: "Now raise your hand if you use some form of maths in everyday life." And more than 80 per cent of the hands go up. How do you bridge the divide? How do you spread the love? How do you raise a generation who will raise their hands for Question Number One, and go on to apply their skills in the workplace? Do the maths. The secret of Maths Centre, love and discipline aside, is a system called Correct, Restore, and Enhance.

The teacher is in her element. She smiles. Her eyes shine. Her hands weave delicately through the air, as if at a loom. She is conquering fear with love. She is explaining how mathematics, first of all, is an alphabet, a series of tools and techniques and operators that are used in the solving of problems. Then there is the way these things connect to the everyday world we live in, to the markets, the clothes we wear, the food we measure and cook and eat. Then there is the power of the teacher, whose job is not just to teach, but to open minds to the vastness of possibility, the magical, spinning infinity of numbers.

"Take the Fibonacci Sequence," says Sharanjeet. The mathematical order of the golden mean that is found in something as simple as the spiral arrangement in the eye of a daisy. Show that to a child. "You don't need to go into any depth. You begin to realise, my goodness me! All of nature is designed around this sequence. Who did it, and when, and what was their plan? Who knows? That is enhancement of mathematics, and I don't see why teachers can't do that. The problem of not doing it, is that you're reducing mathematics to a simple, formal, recipe-driven subject. And it is not."

The greater goal of Maths Centre is to empower learners to see mathematics in the world around them. To see it, even, when they look in the mirror. Sharanjeet once attended a lecture by Nick Binedell, the founding director of GIBS, and the phrase that stuck in her mind, as he spoke about human potential and fulfilment, was: "Everyone should have a map and a mirror." That has worked its way into a Maths Centre programme called Maps and Mirrors, which gives learners an opportunity to navigate their way to a career, by taking a good look at themselves and reflecting on the age-old questions: "Who am I? What am I? What is going to wake me up every day, like Mrs Shan, who can wake up at 4 am at her age, without an alarm clock?" Sharanjeet rises before the dawn, because how else will she see the sun rise on another day? There is so much, at 70, that still needs to be done.

In the two decades since she took up her post, she estimates – and the imprecision troubles her, as a mathematician – that a million learners have in some way been influenced, uplifted, enhanced, by the intersection of their lives with the teachers and programmes of Maths Centre. That is a lot, but it is nowhere near enough. She thinks of the number of children – 50 per cent of the class – who, every year, leave school with zero; no qualification, no prospect of bettering themselves through further education.

She calls it a "haemorrhage", and in the hope of stemming it, she has devised a course and an advocacy campaign that equips learners to venture into artisans' engineering; integrating maths, science, and technology. The project targets learners from Grades 8 to 11, putting them through work experience and the challenges of the engineering world in all its dimensions. One year, the objective was to design and build a tipper truck. "The tipper truck had to perform in a certain way, in terms of carrying a load, and then dumping a load, and so on and so forth," says Sharanjeet. "In that, there is mathematics, inherent science principles, and of course, technology. And about half of those kids from that year decided, 'We are going to stay at school. We don't want to drop out.'"

But it is not just the learners. It is the teachers too. She wants them to feel like leaders. She wants them to feel like achievers. She wants them to leave behind the legacy of a teacher, which is to mould a life and to be remembered. "Nobody remembers a doctor," says Sharanjeet. "Nobody remembers a policeman. Nobody remembers the local greengrocer. But you remember your teacher." Like any good teacher, Sharanjeet has never stopped teaching, and she has never stopped learning.

These days, her greatest teacher is the little girl she calls "my Sotho-Punjabi Princess", her granddaughter, who is nine. She watches her drawing and singing and dancing, she listens to her questions and her thoughts on the world, and she is reminded once again that we are all bundles of energy, fusions of carbon and hydrogen and oxygen, the product of a mathematical formula brought to life. Sharanjeet once won an emerging leader of the year award, and an interviewer asked her what she considered to be her greatest achievement. Without hesitation, she answered: I survived. "I survived and I thrived, against all the odds," she says. "That is my greatest achievement. That I mattered. That I counted. And that is what I want every child to know and believe. That they matter and they count too."

The Social Entrepreneur as an Organisational Leader

K rige (2015) identified common characteristics shared by ten success-ful civil society organisations in South Africa, analysed through the lenses of governance, funding, resource availability and leadership. At the heart of success for these organisations were the leaders, who had developed financial stability for their organisations by adopting social-enterprise approaches, diversifying income streams, and developing "financial security blankets", which allowed the organisations to cover basic costs and/or take risks.

The leaders oversaw well-managed organisations that focused on building trust through accountability, credibility and quality service provision (Krige, 2015). The leaders were largely founder leaders, and had been in position for an average of 12 years.

Blending Business Efficiencies with a Social Mission

Sharanjeet Shan demonstrates many of these characteristics of successful leadership in her approach. She is not the founding leader, but as Krige (2015) notes, it is the leader that is credited with growing the organisation that holds founder-leader status amongst staff and stakeholders. She has held tenure for more than 20 years, significantly longer than the average term of service, and has developed the sustainability of the organisation, evidenced in fact that 15 per cent of Maths Centre's income is brought in through trade and sales, and it has the financial security blanket of owning the building where it is based. Krige (2015) finds that financial independence is one of the key criteria of a successful social organisation, as it separates it from the environment of constraint, creating stability, a degree of predictability and enabling it to take risks.

The model shows how Maths Centre, under Sharanjeet's leadership, has managed to separate itself from the environment of constraint through focussed leadership, financial independence, earning trust through being transparent and accountable, and having a stable mission. Maths Centre is an example of how well-led, professionally-run civil society organisations can naturally transition into the social entrepreneurship environment.

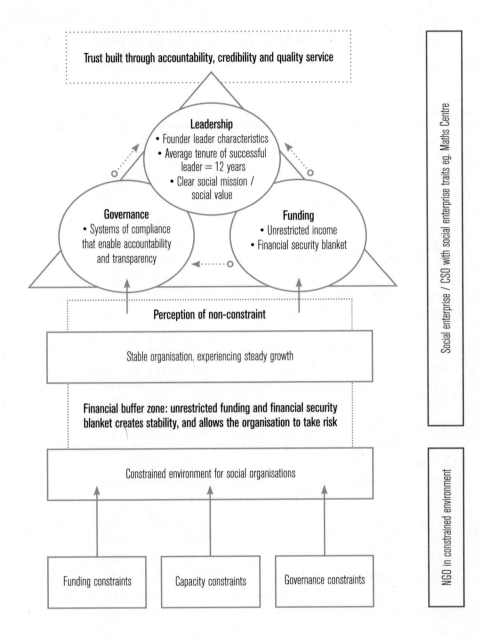

Trust built through accountability, credibility and quality service

Leadership
• Founder leader characteristics
• Average tenure of successful
  leader = 12 years
• Clear social mission /
  social value

Governance
• Systems of compliance
  that enable accountability
  and transparency

Funding
• Unrestricted income
• Financial security blanket

Perception of non-constraint

Stable organisation, experiencing steady growth

Financial buffer zone: unrestricted funding and financial security blanket creates stability, and allows the organisation to take risk

Constrained environment for social organisations

Funding constraints

Capacity constraints

Governance constraints

Social enterprise / CSO with social enterprise traits eg. Maths Centre

NGO in constrained environment

**Maths Centre and Sharanjeet Shan –
a model of success in South Africa**
Adapted from Krige, 2015

ANNE GITHUKU-SHONGWE

A GAME-CHANGER OF THE AFRICAN MIND

Inspired by the sight of her teenage son playing an African hero in a computer game, Anne Githuku-Shongwe is using mobile technology to help young people reimagine a better life, in a better Africa

Anne Githuku-Shongwe walked into her young son's room one day, drawn by the noisy sounds of gameplay coming from his computer. She was about to tell him to turn that off and get back to his schoolwork, when she saw an image on the screen that stopped her in her tracks. Shaka kaSenzangakhona, the Zulu king and warrior, the military genius and tactician who changed the nature of warfare and commanded one of the mightiest nations on the African subcontinent. There he was, proud and strong, in leopard skin, beads, and feathers, an assegai in one hand, a shield in the other, surrounded by the skulls of elephant and buffalo at the gateway to his kingdom. Her son was playing *Civilization*, an American-made strategy game that requires you to "Build an Empire to Stand the Test of Time", by taking on the role of a ruler, a developer, a conqueror. Along the way, you learn the skills of diplomacy, urban planning, technological progress. And a fair bit of history too. Her son, through the magical portal of a computer game, had become an African hero.

For Anne, who was born in the foothills of Nairobi, Kenya, and who now lives in South Africa, it was a moment of hope and revelation. She had wondered often, as a mother of three, a social activist, and a human-development expert working for the United Nations, whether there was a way to make African children look to their own continent for heroes and role models, rather than to the global superstars of Hollywood and TV. The answer: turn the challenge into a game. "I sat there and I thought, what!" she recalls. "Imagine if we could transform this experience into a real experience that could impact on their lives. We use the same medium, make it fun and engaging, but put messages in there that are really important. That is how Afroes was born." Afroes stands for African Heroes and Heroines. It is a digital-technology startup, funded through contracts, grants and public- and private-sector partnerships, that develops mobile games "designed to position youth for success". The flagship game is *Moraba*, modelled on the bottletop boardgame,

Morabaraba, and based on multiple-choice questions on gender violence and sexuality. The player chooses a character, Karabo or Sipho, and answers questions to move bottletops on a board, just as in the real-life version of the game. *Moraba* was inspired by a survey, conducted in the Eastern Cape and KwaZulu-Natal in 2009, that revealed that one in four men had committed sexual violence at least once. Playing the game is meant to challenge myths, stereotypes, and ingrained behaviour. As one young player said, in a feedback session: "Before I played this game, I did not believe I was a rapist. Now I will change my ways."

Then there is *Haki*, a multi-level action game that calls on the player to save villages and fight deforestation. *ChampChase*, backed by the Nelson Mandela Children's Fund, focuses on child safety and security, and provides a platform for children to speak out about abuse. The game was launched during the 2010 FIFA football World Cup in South Africa, at a time when child trafficking was high on the agenda. "It was really about child protection," says Anne. "So you are a real champ in the game, you walk around with a shield on your back and you jump up and down saving these young vulnerable kids from predators. The characters were Themba and Naledi. I remember this one young boy playing the game and he said, 'Ooh, Naledi, Naledi!' He was so excited. Here was a game he could relate to, a name he could recognise." These are games, distributed online or via SMS download codes, promoted through outreach campaigns and community events, that are designed to be fun and easy to play, with hip characters and colourful, noisy graphics. But the greater goal is to "gamify" the big issues affecting young people in Africa, and emancipate them from the mental blocks that thwart their potential and stunt their self-esteem.

> The greater goal is to "gamify" the big issues affecting young people in Africa, and emancipate them from the mental blocks that thwart their potential and stunt their self-esteem.

For Anne, Africa needs a reawakening, and it begins with a renaissance of the imagination. "We want to create a movement of reimaginers," she says. "Our mental models are limiting us." When she told her game-crazy son that she was going to start a company to develop games for Africans, by Africans, his first reaction was: "'You're crazy!' He told his friend that I was going to do this, and he just laughed. He was on the floor. 'Games come from America!' he said. I said to him, we are going to change that story." Anne began building her social enterprise in 2009, making a life-changing decision that brought her mother to tears. For 15 years, Anne had worked as a development professional for the

UN. Now she was about to give all that up to develop games for children to play on their phones. "No, you can't do that!" said her mother. "You have a good career, just hang in there." A friend bet her $1,000 that she would be back at the UN within six months. But Anne, like a character in a game, poised on a clifftop, was ready to take the leap. "I thought, no, I would be really pissed off right now if I died, because of how much of a coward I am, that I can't step out and try something new and different."

The funny thing is, she had learned that attitude from her own mother, who had left a steady job in teaching to become an entrepreneur. "She had a fast-food shop, she sold wholesale household goods to retailers, and she now runs a wholesale second-hand clothing-distribution company." As a teen-ager, together with her brothers, Anne would help her mother run her busi-ness, learning skills of procurement, logistics, stock management, sales and accounting that would later influence her own decision to become an entre-preneur. "Paradoxically, it was my father's work as a Permanent Secretary for Economic Planning, and my desire to impact socio-economic develop-ment, that drove me to economics," says Anne. She studied for a year at the University of Swaziland, before graduating in economics and statistics from St. Lawrence University in the state of New York. She started her career in devel-opment with a policy think tank called Bread for the World, in Washington. In South Africa, it was the era of disinvestment and sanctions, the last gasp of apartheid before the transition to democracy.

Anne had found herself in the midst of the anti-apartheid movement in Swaziland, where her friends at the university included several combatants of the ANC's armed wing, Umkhonto we Sizwe. "Through them," she recalls, "I had a startling awakening to the reality of apartheid and anti-apartheid South Africa." In Washington, Anne became a facilitator, a point of connection at the crux of change, sharing information on South African politics and society with think tanks, universities, churches, Congress lobbyists, and community mobi-lisers. She worked in the American Midwest, driving vast distances through the heartland states of Iowa, Utah, Kansas, Kentucky, and Tennessee, and she was surprised – shocked, even – to learn how curious people were about events taking place at the foot of a continent thousands of kilometres away. "It was shocking to find a whole lot of guys with Stetson hats – cowboys – who were completely informed about South Africa," says Anne. "They knew what was going on. They had views about whether to vote or not vote for sanctions; which way to go. They just wanted an update. What is the latest information, what is going on? Where are the ANC negotiations right now? It was incredible."

She learned a salutary lesson about the way people think, and the way they care, sometimes even more than we care about ourselves in Africa. That point was driven home during a conversation with a government official in Singapore, a regular calling point during Anne's career with the United Nations Development Programme (UNDP). "Why is it that you Africans are willing to give up your destiny?" the official asked Anne. "Your people in leadership are extremely smart, but so mediocre in how they do things. Yet it's your country and your continent's destiny you're gambling with. We succeed because we try. Even if we fail, we still have a mindset of possibility." As Anne pointed out in an essay for the *Huffington Post* in 2014, the greatest return on investment for an African nation would lie not in fixing problems, but in freeing minds. Wherever she would travel on the continent, she would notice a despondency among young people, a sense that their lives were in limbo, that this is where they were stuck, even the brightest among them. It was not a failure of will or ability that she saw. It was a failure of imagination. By the time she settled with her husband in South Africa, to work on regional programmes for the UN, first on HIV and then on innovation and technology, she had a vested interest in helping to improve the lives of young people. She was a mother herself.

> "Why is it that you Africans are willing to give up your destiny?" the official asked Anne…"We succeed because we try. Even if we fail, we still have a mindset of possibility."

"I had given birth to this child," she says, "and when I looked around and started trying to figure out who he will become, there was nothing there to celebrate Africa or Africa's history. I worried about where his values would come from. How would his world be any different from the world of any other person who has grown up in Africa, and is so influenced by the West?" She wanted her children to grow up having heroes, African heroes, and to be unafraid to be heroes themselves. That is why she took the leap, left her job, and started an enterprise of her own. Her first thought, inspired by her son, and the way he had modelled himself on an African king and built a civilisation on his own, was that she could use computer gaming as a platform to reach out to young people, engage them, and get the message across.

Hope, Possibility, Prosperity: the three "mental models" she wanted to instil. Could a young person, living in poverty, imagine the possibility of being prosperous? Could an African child grow up to ride a rocketship to the moon? Could African teenagers hope for a future beyond HIV? She took her cue from an international community called Games for Change, that helps to foster and create "social-impact games" that serve the greater good. The power of games lies precisely in the way they ignite the imagination, stimulate strategic and creative thinking, sharpen reflexes, and transform entertainment into knowledge. They are a storyplaying medium, not just a storytelling medium, and in the right hands, with the right story, they can change hearts, minds, and the world. That, at least, was Anne's hope, as she used a small grant from the Kellogg Foundation to research and develop concepts for games that celebrate African history and heroes.

Her dream was a console video game, epic in scale, that would immerse the player in centuries of action, drama, and learning about the continent and its people. "But when I did the maths, I realised that it is as big as putting together a proper blockbuster movie," says Anne. "A good console game costs between $100 million and $200 million to produce, so I had to temper my super dream. But what I found was that the big console market was an elite, exclusive market of just a few young people who in any case had access to whatever information they wanted, and the real place to find the young people was on mobile." In South Africa, according to a 2012 United Nations Children's Fund (UNICEF) study, 72 per cent of mobile phones are owned by youths aged between 15 and 24. This is the mobile continent, and this is the mobile generation.

In Kenya, on a visit to a rural school, Anne took a quick poll. Raise your hands, she told a class, if you own a mobile phone. Only a few hands shot up. Then she said, how many of you have access to a mobile phone? And every hand in the class went up. Their access was a prepaid SIM card, which they carried in their pockets and slotted into a phone at home or a friend's place. The real African hero: the mobile phone. But a phone on its own is just a phone. To build an enterprise, you need a network. Anne had a friend, Tom Muchiri Kabuga, who was studying a Master of Business Administration (MBA) at Oxford. "He called me and said, I hear you have dared to start trying to do this thing. I said, ja, and he said, okay, well, I am doing my MBA and I need a project to work on. I could come with a group and we can do some thinking. So that was really our first business plan."

Using some of her own savings, Anne hired a small creative and strategic team to work on prototypes. She set Afroes up as a for-profit company, in Kenya and South Africa, because she wanted to create a more sustainable entrepreneurial model for the business. But it has a Non-Governmental Organisation (NGO) component as well, to allow for the channelling of grants. "I wasn't driven by the thought of commercial success," says Anne. "What was more important for me was that we were going to influence the mindsets of people."

With this in mind, Afroes has moved beyond the mechanics of developing and distributing mobile games, into the much broader realm of consulting, licensing content, and offering "complementary life learning" at schools and universities. It has moved beyond education too, to offer advice and guidance on finding a job in the changing world of work. *JobHunt*, for example, is a mobile game that immerses the user in "a virtual world of online work", where the challenge is to compete for jobs, execute them timeously, and earn a living by managing skills and resources. It's just like the real world. But for Anne, the greater challenge is to find a viable, long-term business model for her social-gaming enterprise. "I am creative, I am innovative, I can come up with all kinds of ideas," she says, "but my ideas are stunted by the constant reality of cash flow. The reality of any enterprise is its ability to draw regular revenues and manage cash. I have found that I spend 90 per cent of my time focusing on this rather than on what I enjoy the most, which is to create more products and more impact. I think this has been one of our greatest limitations. There isn't enough serious money and enablement to support ideas to actually grow you to scale."

Anne has a full-time team of eight in South Africa, and three in Kenya. "It is the commitment of the staff to our vision that keeps me going," she says. "I am in tears often. I look at them and think, why? I don't pay you that much. So what is it? Everyone is so driven. Nobody is sitting here thinking, oh, it is time to go home. For me, that is amazing. People make all the difference to any enterprise." In a way, like everything else in life, it is like playing a game. You try, you fail, you win, you lose, you reach the next level, you fall back, you start all over again. And you keep on doing it because you have something greater in mind than the small, fleeting victory. You do it because you want to make a difference, and you want to change people's minds. And that, in its own way, is what it means to be a hero.

The Big Five Traits of a Startup Social Entrepreneur

"I am creative, I am innovative, I can come up with all kinds of ideas," Anne says, and threaded through her story are examples of the personality traits closely associated with startup social entrepreneurs. Personality traits are predictable characteristics that influence how individuals react differently to similar situations (Koe, Nga & Shamuganathan, 2010). In a study that sought to find the link between the Big Five personality traits – openness, extroversion, agreeableness, conscientiousness and neuroticism – and social entrepreneurship, Koe et al. (2010) describe each of the traits and show how they impact the fundamental dimensions of social entrepreneurship. Openness is curiosity; a lack of fear of change. Extroversion is being proactive. Agreeableness is the desire to build consensus and trust. Conscientiousness is the need to maintain high standards, and to work within a set of rules. Neuroticism is having the emotional stability to manage complexity and change (Koe et al., 2010).

How Your Personality Can Affect Your Social Enterprise

Anne possesses all of the Big Five personality traits, to varying degrees. She demonstrates openness in her curiosity, which allows her to see opportunity in the everyday – she identifies an opportunity through watching her son play a computer game. Anne shows extroversion through her ability to take risks when she leaves stable employment on a dare and a $1,000 bet. Her agreeableness is evident in the empathy she has for her team, and in her desire to change mindsets, expanding her work beyond a product to supporting learning in schools and universities. Conscientiousness is ingrained in Anne's childhood – she learns business skills from her mother's entrepreneurial ventures, which she applies as an adult. And, as a typical social entrepreneur, she has a low level of neuroticism, possessing the emotional stability to build an organisation of 11 team members, and to navigate the complexities of a resource-scarce environment.

Koe et al. (2010) theorise that the Big Five personality traits impact the following dimensions of startup social entrepreneurship: social vision, sustainability, social networks, innovation, and financial return. The personality trait that has the biggest impact is openness, which influences all of the dimensions of social entrepreneurship. While conscientiousness impacts only two dimensions, it is vital for sustainability and financial return. Looking at the spectrum from the other side, financial return is impacted by all of the Big Five personality traits, underpinning the complexity of delivering financial surplus. The model maps the personality traits of social entrepreneurs, and how they impact the dimensions of social entrepreneurship.

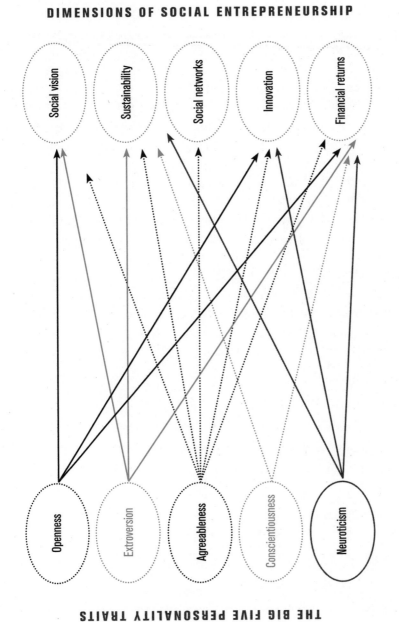

DIMENSIONS OF SOCIAL ENTREPRENEURSHIP

THE BIG FIVE PERSONALITY TRAITS

The impact of the Big Five personality traits on the dimensions of social entrepreneurship

Koe, Nga & Shamuganathan, 2010

NAVIGATING THE GREAT UNKNOWN: STRATEGIES AND APPROACHES OF SOCIAL ENTREPRENEURS

SPARK SCHOOLS

SPARK OF A REVOLUTION

When their MBA lecturer challenged them to think of a way to solve a national crisis, Stacey Brewer and Ryan Harrison put their minds into gear, and came up with a whole new school of thought

Early on a weekday morning, the sun casts its get-up-and-glow on the quadrangle of a primary school in Ferndale, Gauteng. In their uniforms of navy blue and light khaki, worn with sporty white takkies, the children peel themselves away from the clamber gyms and tyre swings, and drift into line on the AstroTurf. They form two loose, chatty battalions, facing each other, with their teachers occupying the gulf in the middle, ready to orchestrate the ritual that kick-starts the day. Like the crackle of a fuse, a quickening trip-beat blares through a speaker, igniting a pledge that booms from a whisper – "I choose, I choose, I choose, to dance, dance, dance, dance" – into a skyrocketing chorus of affirmation: "I throw my hands up in the air sometimes, saying ay-oh, gotta let go!"

The teachers lead by example, shimmying with hands on hips, waving undulating arms, cupping their mouths to shout it all out. The song is "Dynamite", by the British singer Taio Cruz, and you're more likely to hear it at a disco or on a beach than at a school convention. But this isn't a conventional school. It's a SPARK school, part of a network of high-tech independent schools, founded by two GIBS MBA graduates, Stacey Brewer and Ryan Harrison, that aim to make quality private education affordable and sustainable for under-served communities in South Africa.

Beneath the laurel wreath of its logo, capped by a trademark symbol, SPARK is a name that flickers with the energy of a match set to kindling. But it has been engineered into a handy acronym too: Service, Persistence, Achievement, Responsibility, Kindness. The ethos of a new school of thought. As the scholars sling their brightly coloured backpacks onto their shoulders and hurry to class, with the melody of morning assembly lingering like a curlicue in the air, it's clear that learning on these grounds is a lively, upbeat business. In the classroom, where they sit at tables rather than desks, the children are taught basic concepts in small groups, with active discussion encouraged.

Then they move on to laptop-equipped Learning Labs for guided online sessions, using browser-based educational software. A typical school day will include three hours of literacy, 1.5 hours of maths, 40 minutes online, and 40 minutes of physical education. The model, developed and pioneered in the San Francisco Bay Area in America, is called blended learning, and it turns the schoolroom into a place where direct instruction and computer-assisted learning are tightly integrated into the curriculum. So should it be at every school, based on the principle that education must inspire and enlighten young learners, equipping them with the knowledge and skills to construct the livelihoods that will help to build the nation.

But the truth is, the school system in South Africa is in crisis. In a Masters thesis by Stacey Brewer, who graduated cum laude and top of her MBA class at GIBS in 2011, we learn that up to 80 per cent of schools in this country are "dysfunctional", with specific failings in mathematics and literacy. In her graduation year, fewer than a quarter of matric students earned a good enough pass to get into university. And in a 2015 report by the WEF, South Africa was ranked bottom of class, 139th out of 139 countries, for the perceived quality of its science and maths education.

What hope is there for a generation that struggles to read, write, and work with numbers? It's enough to make you throw your hands up in the air, sometimes. But as Stacey gazed into the depths of that crisis, she saw the glimmer of an opportunity. To try and fix the system, to reinvent it from the ground up, to start an enterprise that would make a profit and a difference. Less than a year and a half after handing in her thesis – "A Sustainable Financial Model for Low-Fee Private Schools in South Africa" – she had co-founded SPARK Schools and launched the first SPARK school in Ferndale, with 160 students in Grades R, 1, and 2.

By mid-2015, there would be four schools in the network, with more than 1,000 students and 100 teachers in total. Another four SPARK schools opened in early 2016, in Gauteng and the Western Cape. In the next ten years, the company aims to be running 64 schools, catering for 64,000 students. That's not a learning curve; it's a rocket with its tail on fire, and it suggests a growing demand for educational options outside of free government schooling.

But it also tells a tale of hard work, initiative, vision, chance and timing that began in the age-old way, with a lecturer throwing down the gauntlet to his students. "It was Professor Adrian Saville, who was my first lecturer at GIBS," recalls Stacey. "He was going on about the state of education, and I think you get protected from certain parts of society in South Africa, because I had never realised how bad it was. He started showing us the stats and pretty much challenging us, saying, if you guys are going to be the future business leaders of this country, what are you going to do to sort it out?"

But Stacey also saw the subtext in that challenge, which was: you can't hope to solve this crisis from abroad. You're going to have to stay here, get your hands dirty, and try to make things work. A year ahead of her on the MBA course was Ryan Harrison, a friend from her days at Rhodes University in Grahamstown. She graduated with a Bachelor of Science in Human Kinetics and Ergonomics; he had a Bachelor of Social Science, along with a post-graduate diploma in Media Management.

Like many young South Africans, restless, curious, eager to see the world, they headed overseas after graduation, on what is jokingly known as an LSD: a Look, See and Decide. Ryan worked as a systems analyst in Canada, while Stacey, who admits she has never put her degree to practical use, worked in project management and hospitality. That was enough to land her a job as an onsite manager for a catering company at FIFA headquarters in Sandton, during the hype-and-glory days of the 2010 football World Cup. But her greater goal was to leave home for good.

"I thought, this is my opportunity to get a Masters and then, to be honest, to go back overseas. I went straight into the MBA, and my whole life turned in the opposite direction to what I had imagined." At GIBS, she crossed paths with her prodigal friend, who had managed to secure a small scholarship to study, which he smartly used as collateral for a loan from his dad.

Stacey also saw the subtext in that challenge, which was: you can't hope to solve this crisis from abroad. You're going to have to stay here, get your hands dirty, and try to make things work.

"My dad is a banker," says Ryan. "I think he has had one job and one job interview in his whole life. I said to him, this is a once-in-a-lifetime opportunity, will you allow me to stay at home again and subsidise my fees? He agreed, luckily." As it turned out, the investment paid off. Today Ryan is the Chief Operating Officer (COO) of eAdvance, the holding company of SPARK Schools, and Stacey is the CEO. They sit at a boardroom table in the SPARK school in Bramley in Johannesburg, with bottles of SPARK-branded water in front of them, and it is as if, for once, they have a golden moment to sit back, take a deep breath, and reflect on the road they have travelled.

Ryan wears black trousers and a chequered shirt with the sleeves rolled up. Stacey wears a black skirt and a frilled top, offset by a diamond pendant. Despite being business partners, they are still good friends; despite being good friends, they are still business partners. They are yin and yang, two sides of the same coin, with a calm intensity and a jigsaw of skill sets that has made them an attractive proposition for venture capitalists and corporate funders.

"I don't know how people start companies without a partnership," says Stacey. "It is such a hectic journey and you have your highest highs and your lowest lows. We hope, Ryan and I, that we balance each other out. It is also awesome having a female and male mix, because going into meetings, people respond to us differently, so one can pick up when the other keeps quiet."

They recall an early meeting with a private investor – one of the unexpected benefits of an MBA is that it plugs you into a network of people who know people who know people with money – and he bought in to their vision despite them having nothing to show for it; no proof of concept, just the stirrings of an idea for a school. "We spoke to him for about 15 minutes," says Ryan, "and he obviously saw a spark, I don't know. We didn't even have a name then. He just believed that we needed an investment in education."

> They are yin and yang, two sides of the same coin, with a calm intensity and a jigsaw of skill sets that has made them an attractive proposition for venture capitalists and corporate funders.

The MBA helped, says Stacey. It proved that they were serious about investing in themselves. It helped too that, from the start, they positioned SPARK as a for-profit business. They didn't want to rely on donor money. "If you think about school fees, it is value for money," says Stacey. "We would rather have investors for the long term, who are personally vested to make sure it works, than donors who challenge each mandate. Ryan and I wanted to build something that lives far beyond us, so it is not reliant on us. There was a big push...for profit."

Ryan winces at the notion that there is any inherent incompatibility between the goal of making money and the vision of making the world a better place. "I believe in impact," he says. "I think there is a real problem in the industry, where people fool themselves into thinking that they are saviours of society instead of doing something properly. I think that is very dangerous. At the end of the day, if one rand spent creates impact, then I think you are going to get more impact in a full-profit vehicle."

But back then, in 2011, they were just two students, between careers and opportunities, on the cusp of doing something important with their lives. They were in the same place at the same time, studying the hard science of business administration and the wild art of entrepreneurship. The rest was chemistry, sparked by that professorial challenge – what are you going to do to sort things out? – and the epiphany of the research that opened Stacey's eyes.

In their school days, both Stacey and Ryan attended private colleges, an option that can easily cost parents more than R100,000 a year in fees. But on the other end of the scale, the dysfunction in the state education system has opened up a niche for low-fee private schools that typically charge a tenth of that amount. Operating from office blocks, houses, and inner-city apartments, these schools are largely non-profit, funded by fees, donations in kind, and government subsidies, often registered as tax-exempt Public-Benefit Organisations (PBOs). But they are not a financially sustainable solution to the problem, says Stacey. "A lot of people are just supplementing the system. They are trying to put a Band-Aid over a gaping wound. It is never going to fix it."

As part of her research, she analysed ten private low-fee schools in the Johannesburg area, and found that the average annual cost of educating a child was just over R22,000, almost double the government estimate for educating a child at primary school level at the time of the study. "The big finding was that there was no innovation, and quality was often questionable. Where they would actually save money would be to increase the numbers and pay the teachers less. That wasn't a solution."

Stacey ends her Masters thesis on a note of hope, positing a model for entrepreneurs to innovate and transform education, and provide a better "passport to the future" for the majority of the population in South Africa. That wasn't her answer to Professor Saville's challenge. It was a challenge to herself. Working with Ryan, who had also graduated cum laude, she explored other models of low-fee private schooling in the developing world, including the "slum schools" of Hyderabad, in India, that routinely outperform government schools and have better attendance and resources. But the real answer lay further afield, in the heartland of technology, the epicentre of innovation: Silicon Valley, in California, America. The home of Apple, Adobe, eBay, Facebook, HP, Intel, Twitter, YouTube, Yelp. And Rocketship.

With an introduction from their seed funder, and enough money for six months of research and development, Stacey and Ryan got to know the inner workings of the charter-school network credited with inventing blended learning. Founded by John Danner, a software engineer, and Preston Smith, an elementary school principal, Rocketship opened its first school in 2007, in a church in downtown San Jose. The goal: to provide quality education for the children of low-income and immigrant families, using a model of computer-assisted learning, high-energy rotational teaching, with students moving between spaces and teachers, frequent tests, and a sharp focus on critical thinking and individual data. The school day is longer, too, from 8 am to 4 pm, to allow ample time for "targeted tutoring", gym, and art and music lessons. Today, Rocketship runs 13 schools in three regions, with academic performance consistently in the top five per cent of district schools in California.

The financial model of Rocketship schools is simple. They are free public elementary schools, serving kindergarten through to fifth grade, with government funding topped by donations from wealthy private individuals. But for Stacey and Ryan, the Rocketship model of education was exactly what they had been looking for. Innovative, flexible, scalable, and adaptable.

"It was so exciting because we could really see how it could relate in the South African market," says Stacey. "It completely blew us away. When we came back from the States, we decided, okay, we think we have something here, let's do this full-time. People said it is impossible, there is absolutely no way, you are trying to provide a five-star hotel at three-star prices."

That's where the sustainable financial model comes in. Blended learning drives cost efficiencies, says Stacey. She estimates the annual savings on operations to be R1.6 million per school. With initial private funding of R4.5 million, to run a pilot and launch the first school in Ferndale, SPARK has since had a further two rounds of funding, including a partnership agreement with the Pearson Affordable Learning Fund, part of the UK-based media and education conglomerate.

Parents pay a tuition fee of just over R1,500 per month, and teachers earn above-market rates, says Stacey. Recruitment is a rigorous process, involving four phases, including a sample lesson and an in-depth "mission-and-vision" session, to judge a teacher's fit with SPARK's startup culture. "We look for people who have displayed any kind of excellence in their lives," says Ryan, "whether it is swimming fast or a world record for spinning a coin on their head; anything. If you know what excellence tastes like, you are far more likely to be able to expect it of people."

So, be excellent. Any other advice for aspiring social entrepreneurs? Ryan is quick to answer. "I would say, don't listen to anyone in South Africa. Just don't." Stacey agrees: "Including him!" Her good friend and business partner nods. "Including me. I would genuinely not listen to anyone. I will tell you how we did it, but it may not be right for you. I would say, forge your own path. Take input, but don't take it too seriously. I think if we took input in some of the instances, we definitely wouldn't be doing this." Surround yourself with people who support you, says Stacey. Cheerleaders, people who want you to succeed and who are willing to help. And don't be afraid to speak

openly about your ideas, to share them, as loudly and as often as you can. Nobody is going to steal them from you, because 99 per cent of everything is implementation.

On the whiteboard in the staffroom, a canvas crammed with notes, reminders and thoughts for the day, someone has written a question that has the ring of a challenge: "What was your greatest accomplishment today?" And the answer that stands out, the one that most brings those singing, dancing teachers and their charges to mind, is this: "I smiled throughout the day at my kids, and I meant it."

Opportunity is the Spark of Social Entrepreneurship

For Drucker (2005), identifying and exploiting opportunities is at the heart of entrepreneurial success. Subsequent academic literature has focused on two opposite approaches that enable opportunity: the structured Rational/Economic Approach, and the unstructured style of Effectuation. The Rational/Economic Approach is a goal-oriented process where the outcome is clear from the start, and the entrepreneur takes the steps needed to make this happen. Opportunities are pre-existing, and the entrepreneur "discovers" them. Effectuation recognises how entrepreneurs respond to an idea, using the means available to them, such as their resources, skill, and knowledge, to make it happen. Opportunities are created, and the approach is highly individual, determined by the entrepreneur (Corner & Ho, 2010).

Corner and Ho (2010) identify a spectrum of processes that social entrepreneurs follow to evolve and develop the opportunity, that are more complex than the processes followed by for-profit entrepreneurs. At one end of the spectrum is the Rational/Economic Approach, and at the other end is the free-style Effectuation Approach. Layering the spectrum are the dimensions of life experience (which they call experience corridors), the role of others in making the idea happen (collective action), and the moment the social entrepreneur realises that the kernel of an idea is feasible (spark notion).

Igniting the Rocketship Model

Stacey and Ryan move through the spectrum, germinating their idea through unstructured processes, and then, through research and exposure to the Rocketship model and a venture-capital grant, they shift to a clear vision of the enterprise that they want to build, and the steps needed to get there. They demonstrate collective action in their pairing up, the immediate buy-in of their funding partner, and in the role of their staff who are carefully selected to suit their culture. "I don't know how people start companies without a partnership," Stacey says.

The experience corridor is evident in their motivation to act, beyond the initial professorial gauntlet, and in their valuing of their experience of studying: "I went straight into the MBA, and my whole life turned in the opposite direction to what I had imagined."

The steps taken from original idea to delivery demonstrate the process of spark notion, as the idea evolves and is reframed and tested through experimentation.

Stacey and Ryan's desire to generate social value by tackling the problems of the education system in South Africa shows the typical characteristics of the social entrepreneur in identifying and developing opportunity. Their idea is not discovered or created, it has evolved based on social need, setting them apart from the typical for-profit entrepreneur. This places them in a cycle of opportunity realisation that is both freestyle and constructed.

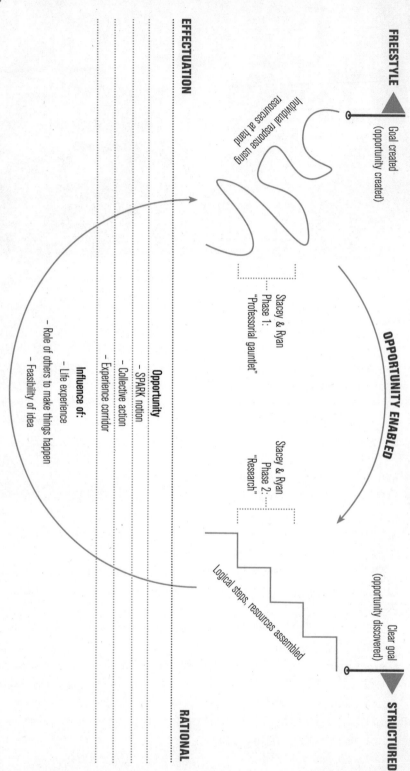

FREESTYLE

Goal created
(opportunity created)

EFFECTUATION

Individual response using
resources at hand

Stacey & Ryan
Phase 1:
"Professorial gauntlet"

Opportunity
– SPARK notion
– Collective action
– Experience corridor

Influence of:
– Life experience
– Role of others to make things happen
– Feasibility of idea

OPPORTUNITY ENABLED

Stacey & Ryan
Phase 2:
"Research"

Clear goal
(opportunity discovered)

STRUCTURED

Logical steps, resources assembled

RATIONAL

The freestyle and structured cycle of opportunity recognition
Based on Corner & Ho, 2010

NEIL CAMPHER

TURNING WASTE INTO WORTH IN HELENVALE

In a neighbourhood notorious for gangsterism and violence, Neil Campher is leading the drive to recycle despair into hope

In Helenvale, north of Port Elizabeth, where the wind carries the bitter sting of history as it whips in from the seafront, Neil Campher once saw a man sitting at a concrete block, chipping away with a hammer. A tractor, hauling a trailer full of garbage and rubble, had struck the block a glancing blow, exposing the core of metal at its base. Neil, who runs the Helenvale Recycling Initiative (HERI), a campaign to turn "waste into worth" in the area, drove over to assess the damage. He greeted the man, and paused to watch him at work. Tap tap tap.

The cement flew off in fragments, the shrapnel of a backbreaking task that looked like a form of penance. Like a miner, the man was working his way through to the metal, which he planned to sell to a scrap dealer for a few rand. "How long do you think that will take you?" asked Neil. "As long as it takes," said the man. "Even if I have to sit here the whole day." Sometimes, it can be difficult to tell the difference between persistence and desperation. But in that act of relentless drudgery, Neil saw a glimmer of hope, an ideal of positive consequence trapped in the ore.

If people were prepared to invest so much physical effort for such little return, what wouldn't they do to better their lot in life? What if you could find a way to channel that energy, to multiply it, to kick-start a revolution in the way people see themselves, each other, and the place they call home? You have to be an activist to think like that. You have to be an optimist, a believer in the virtuous cycle of behaviour as a driver of change. But more than anything, whatever it takes, you have to be prepared to go to Helenvale and back to make a difference.

Neil is a jovial, engaging man, a natural persuader and connector, with glasses and an impish grin. Until a few years ago, he was more at home in the boardroom, as the Executive Director of investment-holdings group Ukuvula, a group with interests in industrial machinery, automotive components, and medical supplies. He now runs his own social-innovation and enterprise-training consultancy, through which he works to "contribute positively and imaginatively towards building sustainable communities".

He studied sales and marketing at university, and began his working life in container logistics at a shipping company, but at heart, he has always seen himself as a social entrepreneur, harnessing his business and technical acumen to help communities help themselves. In Helenvale, he works at the grassroots, hoping to convince people that the grass will be greener when you pull out the weeds and clear away the rubbish. Recycling is a metaphor. It is an act of cleansing that binds a community, through hard, honest toil that produces tangible, visible results. In Fitchard Street, there was an illegal dumping site, one of many in Helenvale, where brightly coloured bags of garbage lay festering. A garden of flotsam and jetsam that grew higher and higher, until you could only wade through it.

> He works at the grassroots, hoping to convince people that the grass will be greener when you pull out the weeds and clear away the rubbish. Recycling is a metaphor. It is an act of cleansing that binds a community, through hard, honest toil that produces tangible, visible results.

Today it is a communal park, surfaced with neatly raked gravel, a clamber wall of painted tyres, shrubs and saplings, and concrete benches to sit on. People come here to watch their children play ball. They come to braai and gossip and hold al fresco prayer meetings. They have reclaimed a part of their neighbourhood that once was sterile and dead, a hazard to health and happiness. Of course, there is money in the metaphor too. There is Auntie Martina, for example, who marshals a helper to collect junk from shops and shebeens, and stores it in a shack next to her house.

"They sort it and then they sell it to a trader who comes around and gives them a price," says Neil. "She makes roughly R250 to R350 a week." There are the primary and high schools, with their recycling clubs and their timetable for accumulating assorted species of refuse: paper, cardboard, and groceries on Monday, plastic on Wednesday, tin cans on Friday. Hillcrest Primary, once a landmark because of the illegal dump just across the road, is now a landmark because of its monumental achievement: "In one day," says Neil, "they brought in 1,600 kilograms of recyclables. It took us two weeks to clear the quad of all the stuff." The schools earn roughly R300 a week.

There is value in waste, but the real dividend is a shift in perceptions, in the way people see themselves and the way the world sees them. Helenvale, says Neil, slipping with ease into the lexicon of the PowerPoint deck, is an operating environment burdened by negative brand equity. It is a community shaped and defined by the trauma of forced removal, and the ruthless cycle of social ills, dependency, and violence. Its other name, the label it wears like a curse, is Katanga, borrowed from the war-torn region of the Democratic Republic of Congo, where villagers live in fear of bands of marauding rebel troops.

"When people think of Helenvale," says Neil, "generally speaking, they look at it as a dark force. It is the most written-about, most talked-about, most dangerous, most derided community in the whole province." The war here is against gangsterism, crime, domestic violence, drug and alcohol abuse, poverty, overcrowding, and unemployment, affecting mainly women, and youth, who make up 69 per cent of the population.

But it is a war against the past too, a legacy of disconnection and abandonment that keeps returning, like the tide. The beachfront of Port Elizabeth, the Friendly City of the Eastern Cape, with its luxury hotels, holiday playgrounds, gracious sandstone monuments, and rows of terraced Victorian houses, lies just 15 kilometres to the south. It is a city of easygoing charm, stirred from its languor by the blustering trade winds that call every now and again from across the Indian Ocean. But it is only when you leave the shelter of the bay, and you slip off the freeway onto Stanford Road, that you begin to see the effects of a greater force of nature, the hurricane of social change that swept people away and corralled them according to their race during the heyday of Grand Apartheid.

These are the Northern Areas, a sprawl of townships between the salt pan and the harbour, representing more than 250,000 people in 40 neighbourhoods and 11 ward councils. Helenvale is the epicentre, the trigger point, of their systemic failure to thrive. Built to accommodate 6,000 people, in subdivided concrete houses that were only fitted with electricity and indoor sanitation in the post-apartheid era, Helenvale today has a population of about 21,000, according to the Mandela Bay Development Agency.

To cope with the overspill, almost 80 per cent of homes have a shack made of timber or corrugated iron in the backyard. Unemployment is as high as 75 per cent, and the average household income is just over R2,700 a month, based largely on casual labour and government grants for disability and child support. This is a youthful township, with almost two-thirds of the population under the age of 35. But only one in ten has a matric, the basic criterion for tertiary study and the prospect of a professional career.

There are 49 streets in Helenvale, the prowling ground of gangs, with easy access to drugs and weapons: the Dustlifes, the Upstand Dogs, the Untouchables, the Boomshakas, and the Shootas. "Sometimes during school, we hear shots fired at the perimeter fence," says Malcolm Roberts, principal of Helenvale Primary School. "We have developed a system with students, who must go into classrooms when they hear the shots. This is not the ideal environment for children to learn."

And yet, for the activist, the optimist, the believer, Helenvale is a testing ground for revival, a reason to look to the light, roll up your sleeves, and get down to work. Neil grew up around here, in the more sedate working-class neighbourhood of Korsten, the son of an educator who later became a bus driver and conductor. Neil remembers Helenvale, with some irony, as a place of refuge: "We used to go and hide there for two reasons. One was leisure, and the other was safety. As young people, persecuted by the South African Police back in the day, we knew it was a safe place, because the police wouldn't want to go in there."

It was a no-man's land, and the lawlessness did not cease when apartheid ended. In 2011, with Neil as co-founder, a collective of civil society volunteers called the Northern Areas People Development Initiative (NAPDI) convened to address the challenges and find ways of overcoming them. The catalyst was the killings of 21 young people in drug wars and gang violence in just four months of that year. To begin with, NAPDI did nothing but listen: to parents and children, scholars, unemployed youth, family and church groups, and sports, business, and cultural organisations.

From this public process flowed an in-depth report – "Living, Working, Learning, Praying and Playing in the Northern Areas" – and a set of four scenarios calibrated on the North Star. Scenario planning is not the science of foretelling the future. It is a way of telling stories that can determine the pathway to the best of all possible tomorrows. There are always the worst cases, the roads fraught with peril, the journeys you seek to avoid. Here they included the Shooting Star, a future of weak economic development that leads to nowhere, fast, and the Fallen Star, where poor leadership and low morals and ethics confine the community to a dead zone. Then there was the Bright Star, which would depend on strong and capable leadership, a focus on youth and development, and a common purpose illuminated by the guiding mantra: "I see the light".

The scenarios were outlined in 2012, and part of the exercise included imagining headlines in the community newspapers of 2022. For Bright Star, they would read: "Drug dealers agree to back off, residents take war to drugs"; "Return to values drives renewal in Northern Areas"; "Five hundred Northern Areas learners enter university"; "Northern Areas learner attains eight distinctions"; "Police in Northern Areas among best in country"; and "Nelson Mandela Bay Municipality awarded international peace prize for Northern Areas visionary initiative".

It is always good to aim for the stars. But in the real world, the hard work begins a lot closer to Earth. A synopsis of the original NAPDI document found its way to the desk of Noxolo Kiviet, then-Premier of the Eastern Cape. Her office had identified one problem symptomatic of the trouble with the region: the illegal rubbish dumps of Helenvale. Neil got a call, a request for further information, and along with it a challenge, a test of commitment, on a pathway paved with good intentions. "Could you put together a proposal?"

There was funding attached, a modest initial amount of R1 million, which would later be supplemented by grants from Coca-Cola and the Ubutyebi Trust, a private NPO. "The concept was very simple," says Neil. "We just said, let's get together and work with the people of Helenvale." In July 2012, HERI was launched, as a priority intervention project on behalf of the Premier. In the best-case scenario, Bright Star, the NAPDI planners had hinged their vision on a socio-economic model of an "engaged community". On a graph, they had plotted a possible pathway to redemption. The horizontal axis was the level of leadership, good or bad, and the vertical axis was the level of economic participation by the community.

"We used that as a guide, and came up with a concept that said, look, if the problem is illegal dumping, it's one thing to do a clean-up campaign, but it is another to look at the mindset of people. If the smorgasbord of challenges was so wide, why would you tackle a thing like illegal dumping? So we put together a proposal that spoke to recycling as a trigger." Recycling was doable and necessary, says Neil, but the bigger goal was to use it as a springboard for sustainability, a way of transferring and developing skills that would draw Helenvale closer to the glow of that bright and distant star: the Best-Case Scenario.

There were 75 illegal dumps in Helenvale, scattered through the neighbourhood, an eyesore and a symbol of the misery of the Group Areas Act, the apartheid edict that uprooted neighbourhoods and fractured community life. But fixing the problem was going to take a lot more than a convoy of trucks and a battalion of eager volunteers with gloves and garbage bags. For one thing, the municipal waste collectors were not at all keen to drive into Helenvale.

"Their trucks would be hijacked by gangsters who would take the thing on a joy ride," says Neil. "They would damage the thing and they would rob the guys of their watches and their clothes, and then drive off. If people from the outside were not even prepared to come in, why would anyone from the area want to do something?" But the bigger problem was that the illegal dumping was not necessarily a symptom of antisocial behaviour or a reckless disregard for hygiene. It was a form of public protest against a system that was itself seen to be a rampant waste of resources.

The municipality had replaced the plastic garbage bags used by house-holds with wheelie bins, which were supposedly more efficient and environmentally friendly. "But the worst is, they reduced garbage collection from once a week to once every two weeks, because you wouldn't have plastic bags, so everything would be in the bin. That was the logic, and it backfired spectacularly." In a case study of unintended consequence, the wheelie bins, discarded as receptacles, became prized commodities instead, sought after as forms of transport for goods to trade, and for the scrap value of the iron rods that connect their wheels.

> Neil believed the campaign would have a less than five per cent chance of succeeding, if it followed the standard practice of prescription and imposition from an outside agency. The community had to self-organise. They had to affirm and manage their participation.

Neil stopped at a shebeen one day to speak to people about the recycling initiative, and he saw a man pulling a wheelie bin, scraping it along the ground, down an incline. It had no wheels. It was loaded with scrap metal from a roofing project. "I asked him, *boet*, where are you going? He told me he was going to sell it. I asked him how much he was going to get for it, and he said, R10, maybe R15 if I am lucky, depending on the weight and the quality." Already, in Helenvale, there was an ethos of recycling, of salvaging, even if it was often negative entrepreneurship, which is the working definition of criminal activity.

"They were stealing stuff," says Neil. "They would have been pulling cords out of the public lights to get to the copper. Anything that was worth selling. So this was a selling community." But that wasn't a solution; that was part of the problem. Neil believed the campaign would have a less than five per cent chance of succeeding, if it followed the standard practice of prescription and imposition from an outside agency. The community had to self-organise. They had to affirm and manage their participation.

A psychologist who worked on the project once told Neil that there was a veil around Helenvale. "What people see from the outside is not what we see from the inside. What we need to do is take this veil off, and reveal the truth about what is happening behind it." The breakthrough was the creation of a framework for the community to discover its own truths, to draw on its own strengths. There is a process of social activation called Asset-Based Community Development (ABCD). It is a methodology that shifts the emphasis from solving specific problems to creating meaningful change by focusing on "local assets": in this case, the people of Helenvale.

A team of 50 HERI Challenge Team ambassadors, mostly young, unemployed women, selected from 250 respondents, were kitted out with branded tee shirts, equipped with pens and writing pads, and dispatched into the neighbourhood in search of "positive community stories". What they found, beyond the trauma and social upheaval, was the true face of Helenvale. A face of civic pride, compassion, mutual support and upliftment.

They met the Eyethu Peace Workers, who fight crime with street patrols. They met the reformed gangsters who were steering impressionable youngsters away from the thug life. They heard about Oom Ronnie and Auntie Katie, who run a soup kitchen. They heard about Auntie Audrey, who breathes with a ventilator, and who donates part of her pension to the needy. They heard about the good work of churches, schools, and the scout pack with its brass band. They saw Helenvale, anew, as a place where people stand together to promote hope. And then, with the help of volunteers, they took to the streets to clean them up, turning dumpsites into play sites, filling bag after bag with garbage, planting the seeds for a shift of mindset that could be measured by the tonne.

By September 2013, a year and two months after the launch of HERI, more than 4,000 tonnes of waste had been removed and trucked to landfill. "That is roughly 400 ten-tonne tipper trucks," says Neil.

There have been obstacles too. Where there is garbage, there is politics. Helenvale is run by the Democratic Alliance (DA), and the local branch of the ANC accused the clean-up campaign of being a DA initiative, despite it being a priority project of the Premier's office. "They issued a letter of demand, a year after we started, saying they wanted the project out of Helenvale," says Neil.

He was warned, too, to stay away from certain dumpsites, because they were used by gangsters to stash drugs. But one day, he stopped to talk to a group of gangsters who were acting as enforcers of a different kind. Their turf included a spotlessly clean alleyway. "They were enforcing cleanliness, making sure no one threw any rubbish there," says Neil. "I congratulated them for their efforts."

Today the recycling initiative is a subset of a broader campaign called Safety and Peace through Urban Upgrading, which is funded by a 5-million Euro investment from the German Development Bank. That international peace prize, envisioned by the scenario planners, may still be a distant dream, but the real newspaper headlines have been reward enough: "Helenvale area cleans up its act"; "Heavenly makeover for Helenvale"; "Making a difference to poor in Helenvale".

Neil is regarded in the neighbourhood as a man who cares about Helenvale, and who doesn't easily take no for an answer. "When Neil came to me first, I was sceptical," says principal Malcolm Roberts. "You want us to do what? With rubbish? But he is very persistent, and so we got this waste project going. It started off really slowly, but Neil is the guy who keeps hammering at things. He doesn't give up. His persistence is infectious."

The local DA ward councillor, Nico du Plessis, credits Neil for his diplomacy, his skill as a connector: "He has managed to get people from different political spheres into one room, and the mindset has changed. He is very positive, and he knows what he's doing. I don't just like him because he grew up in front of me; I like him because he thinks out of the box."

But for Neil, if the project has worked at all, it has worked because it is not his project. It belongs to the people of Helenvale. "If you really want to solve a problem," he says, "you have to hand it over to the community. You have to walk the journey with them. You have to give the campaign the best possible chance, by having the first positive experience from the community's side. If they can see it, if they can affirm it, then your job is halfway done."

In 2008, two Masters students in spatial planning from the Blekinge Institute of Technology in Sweden, Emely Lundahl and Nina Södergren, presented a proposal for the upgrading of Helenvale. They called it "Yesterday, Today, Tomorrow". Their artist's impressions show a neighbourhood that is clean and well-lit, with children playing in parks, and trees lining walkways and broad boulevards. The houses are bright and spacious. The community centres and business areas are safe. It no longer looks like a dream, a mere thesis of possibility. The Bright Star is on the horizon. The glint of metal is in the ore. You just have to keep believing, and you just have to keep hammering away.

A Champion of the Asset-Based Community Development Approach

ABCD challenges the needs-based approach to social development. Instead of focusing on needs, communities identify their strengths, enabling them to make decisions that build on existing resources (Mathie & Cunningham, 2003). This heightened accountability to constituents and the outcomes created is one of the classic defining characteristics of a social entrepreneur (Dees, 2001). ABCD is an approach that enables the community to lead, by following a set of processes:

- comprehensively mapping the assets of the community
- mobilising a core group of community organisers
- initiating activities within the community that don't require outside assistance
- progressively scaling up these initiatives as external links are made (Mathie & Cunningham, 2003).

One of the early activists of asset-based thinking, Canadian educator Moses Coady (1959) writes: "Bringing life to the people means getting them first of all to see the possibilities…when people see possibilities, they will more or less instinctively try to translate them to actuality."

Neil is a champion of ABCD. His role in the community is not to set up an enterprise or run a project that delivers change, but rather to encourage people to take up an idea – in this case recycling – to catalyse their collective vision. Neil's role is as a connector and facilitator, who recognises that the community has to self-organise if the recycling campaign is to work.

The ideas for change have emerged through an extensive community engagement process that mapped the community's thoughts and visions for the future. Neil follows this up by selecting 50 community activists who continue to engage with the community, collecting feedback that talks of "civic pride, support and upliftment", resulting in a massive volunteer response that collects 4,000 tonnes of waste in its first effort. The intervention is community driven and led, building up to involve schools, co-operatives, and the steady and sustained restoration of parks and recreation areas. In line with Mathie and Cunningham (2003), Neil is able to connect the community externally, to the local development agency, securing a substantial infrastructure grant to continue the community's momentum.

An Instinctive Broker of Social Change

As a social entrepreneur, Neil has instinctively stepped into the role of broker, which is often required to activate social capital. He is able to navigate the tensions and power fluctuations of community life, while taking an "arms-length role" that is flexible and attuned to community interests (Mathie & Cunningham, 2003, p. 11). The result is a sustained change in the attitude of community members to their environment, and a successful lobby for infrastructure funding from provincial government. As the model opposite shows, Neil has successfully achieved the goals of asset-based development: "Activity based at the community level, conducive to building active participation in, and a sense of responsibility for, the prosperity of the larger community" (Mathie & Cunningham, 2003, p. 10).

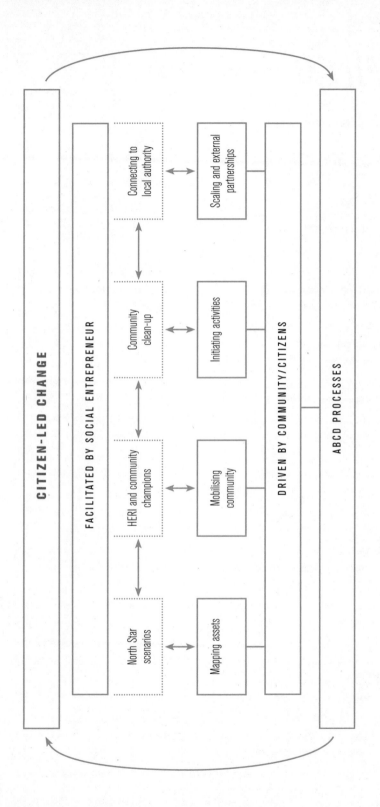

Neil's work in Helenvale: using ABCD processes to catalyse change

Based on Mathie & Cunningham, 2003

PAT PILLAI

LIFE IS A TEACHER

Beyond the mountain, beyond the scrubland of his home on the Flats, Pat Pillai saw the glimmer of a better way. And then, learning to teach, teaching to learn, he turned his vision into an enterprise for life

The young man stood in the queue outside the admin block of the University of Durban-Westville, waiting to enrol for the degree that he hoped would qualify him to be a teacher. He had travelled up by train from his home on the Cape Flats, where he lived in a garage – a double garage, at least – with his five younger siblings and his parents. There was a short-pile carpet, navy blue weave, and sometimes the light would shine through from the holes in the roof, and fall in little shimmering pools. It was like having the stars come to play in your home. He grew up thinking that there was a giant tunnel in the middle of Table Mountain, and all you had to do was drive through it to get to the north. He didn't know much about the world. But he did know that you had to dress smartly for your first day at varsity, and so he was wearing his best shirt and trousers and a pair of shiny shoes. But the other young men, so cool and care-free, were wearing tee shirts and takkies and jeans with holes at the knees. I may as well have dressed the way I dress on the Flats, he thought to himself.

That wasn't the only thing that set him apart. Standing in the queue with him, making sure he was all right, was his 80-year-old grandfather, who all his working life had waited on tables, rising eventually to the pinnacle of his profession: Head Waiter at the Grandest Hotel in the World, the Mount Nelson in Cape Town. But for the young man, this was a source of shame rather than pride. He had wondered, throughout his teenage years, how his grandfather could happily have served powerful, often openly racist white people, when by law, because of the colour of his skin, he was not allowed to sit and eat at the tables himself.

Thatha, thought the young man, I wish you weren't here with me now. He took a number and went to wait on the grass. His grandfather sat on a bench, and took out a flask of tea and sandwiches wrapped in wax paper. Thick slices of brown bread, with braised cauliflower and peas and dollops of butter. They ate, in silence. Then the old man said, "Patmanathan, you

must never be ashamed of where you come from. I know you are ashamed of me." In that moment, the young man's world turned inside out. He saw that the grandfather who loved him unconditionally felt abandoned, alone on a campus that he too was visiting for the first time in his life. In his selfish discomfort, the young man felt he had betrayed his *Thatha*. His shame was washed away by guilt and a fresh perspective. He joined the queue again after lunch, proud now to be the only student on campus with his beloved grandfather at his side.

> Life is full of lessons that we learn from doing things wrong. We share them, in the hope that others may do things right.

Life is full of lessons that we learn from doing things wrong. We share them, in the hope that others may do things right. Our memory, our heritage, keeps us anchored to our roots, drawing us back no matter how far we may rise. Patmanathan Danaventhan Sockalingam Pillai. That was the young man's name. Today he is better known as Pat Pillai, who read the news on TV, suave and good-looking, with a voice that resonated with calm and trust. An anchor. But what he really is, what he always wanted to be, is a teacher.

"I am a teacher first," he says. "You have to find some structure around you to make sure you can do what you love. I love stories, and I love what I do." The structure around him is an NPO called LifeCo UnLtd South Africa, born from Pat's model for teaching young people what they may not have been taught in school. How to communicate, how to be confident, how to be a leader, how to be an entrepreneur. How to uplift yourself, and uplift others, without ever forgetting where you come from.

"We want to reach one million youth, grow 100,000 leaders, and build an asset base of R500 million by 2020," says Pat. LifeCo UnLtd is fully owned and governed by a trust, which in turn owns 100 per cent of a diversified investment company. All its proceeds are invested in its social mission. "Our mission happens to be building life champions who, regardless of circumstances, will find a way."

Pat found a way. He sits in the boardroom of the LifeCo Country Campus in Fourways, Johannesburg, wearing a narrow-lapelled suit jacket, and beneath that, a black tee shirt emblazoned with an orange-and-silver logo, like flames around his heart. His neatly trimmed beard is speckled with grey. He projects the quiet authority of a teacher commanding a class.

He is 50 now, and he remembers how it all began, when he was 23, with a degree, but nothing you would call a steady job, and he was holding his newborn child in his arms, taking care of the 2 am feed. He felt the weight of destiny, the mantle of responsibility, as the first-born son of a first-born son of a first-born son. And now, he too had a son he had to look after, to shape and mould and set free into the world.

"I felt inept as a father. I felt inept as a teacher," he says. "I knew that what he needed was more than I was qualified to deliver." Pat had escaped the Cape Flats, the wind-whipped stretch of scrubland on the wrong side of the mountain, where entire communities, uprooted and displaced by apartheid, had been left to start again. But he had not been able to escape the prison of his mind.

"I recognised that the education system did nothing with the real challenge I had, which was my dependency mentality," says Pat. "My internal enslavement. I knew, late at night, that I was probably going to impose the same psychosocial programming on my son, and not even know what the hell I was doing." Pat had a brother who was involved with drugs, and another who was intensely violent. His mother, who had only had a Standard 4 (Grade 6) education, would walk kilometres to bring home the groceries, with the small change she earned from waitressing and other odd jobs. His father, short-tempered, with a violent streak too, was a printer who was often out of work. Pat wanted to break out of the cycle. He wanted to teach.

He knew a playwright who ran a community theatre and a nightclub, close to the campus of the University of Durban-Westville. Pat went to see him, with the idea of running classes – life classes – to supplement the formal skills that were being taught at school. He placed an ad in a paper, and a few parents turned up to hear what he had to say. He called the school the Vaughn Antony Creative Arts Project, after the son he had held in his arms at 2 am. He wanted to open doors for other children too. The venue for the classes was the nightclub.

"You do not want to see what the dance floor of a nightclub looks like with the lights turned on," says Pat. But he had a small class and a premise of redemption – *emancipate yourself from mental slavery* – and it was enough to earn him a modest keep for a few months. The real jolt, the shining light of truth, was the realisation that he was going to have to be his own first student.

"My economic model was a complete mess," says Pat. "There was an intention, and there was a conversation, but the curriculum was very poorly thought-out. It was a failure, because I made promises to parents, and didn't follow through. I had to go back to school to learn how to put an enterprise together, to sustain the promise."

But in the glare of that nightclub, the seed of an idea had taken root. Education, nurtured into blossom by drama. As a teenager, Pat had suffered from an irregular stutter, aggravated by uncontrollable blinking that mimicked his efforts to make himself understood. At the time, it was diagnosed as a side effect of his epilepsy, although he now says, strong and clear of voice, "it was all in the bloody mind". He had his first seizure at high school. It came out of nowhere. He woke up on a bed in the sickbay. "The most embarrassing thing was, my shoes were taken off, my tie was gone and my collar had been loosened, and all I could see was my toe sticking up out of a hole in my sock." He should have listened to his mother when she said, darn it. Another lesson for life.

He was treated at the Red Cross Children's Hospital, and someone said, keep him away from flashing lights and stressful situations, such as speaking in public. "I listened to this – I was 14 – and my mother listened to it, and I remember thinking, '*Wat se kak?*' I want to be a teacher, and teachers have to stand in front of a class and speak. It didn't sit nicely. My mom said, 'Patmanathan, listen, be a good boy.'" Pat didn't listen. For ten years, after getting his degree, he ran an enterprise called South African Theatre Common. It was a travelling theatre group that put on plays at schools, shining a spotlight of epiphany on the dry data, difficult works, and abstract concepts in the syllabus.

"Some person would say, I am battling with algebra, my kids are not getting it," says Pat. "So I would find a way to dramatise *a* multiplied by *b*. I helped students better understand clouds and rocks. Some plays dealt with life, stories of our struggle. I would use gumboot dance to demonstrate rhythms and principles of life. It wasn't always to do with the human condition. There was no Google then, so I would pick up all these lovely ideas and try them out in class. I had the students standing on their desks, and running outside in the rain, and of course the parents would complain. But I made a living out of it. I fed my family."

He would charge the school R3 a ticket, and keep R2 for himself, with the remaining R1 going to the school fund. He was visiting ten schools a week, and reaching about 1,000 students per school. "It grew to a point where I was in three of the four provinces at the time." And that was only because, as he notes, Indians weren't allowed to stay or trade in the Orange Free State during apartheid. South Africa was a theatre of the absurd, and Pat was a performing artist with his name up in lights. But he was a teacher first, and once again he went back to school, this time to learn about lighting, because if you can't get cast in a show, they're still going to need someone to rig the lights. "Suddenly I had work all the time," he says.

Then, in 1990, came the dawn. The release of Nelson Mandela, the unbanning of political organisations, the slow and uneasy shuffle to democracy. The SABC, the national broadcaster, had to reinvent itself as a platform for all the people. And there was Pat, playing a new role in front of the camera, first as a sportscaster on TopSport Surplus – "What do I know about sport? Even less than I do about teaching!" – and then, perfectly cast, as a presenter on a documentary and educational channel called NNTV.

In Adrian Steed, the urbane TV and radio anchor, with the flawless diction and the voice as soothing as balm, he found a mentor, from the old school to the new. "Remember," he told Pat, "whenever you are broadcasting, no matter how many people are out there, you are only ever speaking to one person." And then, the age-old advice: "Be authentic. Never forget where you came from." Wisdom is an echo. The words of Sockalingam Pillai, Pat's grandfather, whose name he wears in his name, like a badge of pride, come drifting down through the years. Pat remembers. He grew up in a garage with holes in the roof, but when he restarted Life College in 1997, for all the distance he had travelled, that was in a garage too. Auntie Hawa's garage in Lenasia, a tradition-ally Indian suburb, south of Johannesburg.

"She was a warm, jovial, soft-spoken Muslim woman of Malaysian descent," says Pat. "She had a home across the road from a school we supported. She was very kind to us. We insisted that we wanted to pay, but she refused. Even when we tried to slip some money under the door, what we got back in samoosas and tea far out-weighed it." He had saved a bit of money over the years, enough to fund what he hoped would be a school that could run parallel to the school system. A school of life.

"We...went door to door, like Tupperware salesmen. We would quickly say, we are here to talk to you about your child. When you say you are a group of teach-ers, somehow people listen."

Then Carmen de Rito joined. She too is a teacher, and immediately saw the potential to impact society through business-centred, value-added educa-tional and entrepreneurial programmes. LifeCo UnLtd's co-founder was on board. At the time, earning just R500 a month, Carmen got to work and built the content, systems, and operational rigour that still underpins the national-scale rollout. "There would be no LifeCo UnLtd without Carmen," says Pat. Pat and Carmen signed up a few part- and full-time teachers.

"We distributed flyers at street corners and went door to door, like Tupper-ware salespeople. We would quickly say, we are here to talk to you about your child. When you say you are a group of teachers, somehow people listen. We said, would you trust us to train your child? To build their self-confidence and enhance their outlook? If we don't do a good job, we may even give your money back." They did a good job. To start with, there were 16 students. The parents were paying R190 a quarter, by debit order, and their children were taught after hours, in rented classrooms.

"We never raised a single cent by donation," says Pat. "And then, sometime in 2003, someone came along and said, you are doing such good work, we would like to donate money. We had a problem. I said, I can't take your money, I don't know how to account for it. We cannot give you a certificate. They said, okay, you better register something, and we did. We registered as an NPO." They called it SA Life College. But you never really graduate from life; you just get better at dealing with it. "With the skills you learn, maybe you can land a job, or start a company of your own, and create other jobs in turn," says Pat. "And you never stop learning. That is a special skill in itself. A dynamic way of thinking that is not always taught in schools."

> You never really graduate from life; you just get better at dealing with it. "With the skills you learn, maybe you can land a job, or start a company of your own, and create other jobs in turn," says Pat. "And you never stop learning."

That premise appealed to loveLife, an NGO that promotes and develops leadership and healthy lifestyles among young people. They approached Life College and said, here's a cheque for R50,000. Train our leaders. "We jumped up and down for joy," says Pat. "We couldn't sleep. We framed the cheque."

Today, it is not unusual for Life College, now known as LifeCo UnLtd, to be paid R5 million a year for implementing a development programme for a school, university, or other organisation; or issue an invoice for R25 million to find, fund, and support social entrepreneurs. "We earn our keep," says Pat. "We trade for change, we don't beg for small change. Only about five per cent of our annual budget is donated. We are proud that LifeCo UnLtd is 100 per cent owned by a social trust, and we buy stakes in values-aligned, high-growth, profitable businesses. All dividends and profits fund our social mission."

The aim is to build a nation of champions, but that is naïve, beautifully naïve, says Pat. You can't put 50 million people in a classroom, give them capital, and turn them into entrepreneurs. The best you can hope for is a percentage, a tipping point of the right people in the right communities. After 18 years of implementation, LifeCo UnLtd has reached over 80,000 people, 4,000 of whom have started micro enterprises and 108 of whom have gone on to start formal businesses, with annual turnovers ranging from R100,000 to R5 million. LifeCo UnLtd was voted among the top ten most-trusted social enterprises in South Africa in the Ask Africa Survey, 2011.

"There is work to be done. Entrepreneurship is a state of mind. A confidence in self and enterprise," says Pat. "There have been failures; too many. Some of them emerge simply knowing they are not entrepreneurs. Some emerge very clear that they are, but confused as hell as to what they are going to do. But they all grow."

Look at Pat. If you were to ask him, as the founder and CEO of an enterprise with a turnover of R25 million and an asset base of R110 million, whether he considers himself to be a social entrepreneur, he will smile and say, no, of course not. He is a teacher. Patmanathan Danaventhan Sockalingam Pillai, from Rylands on the Cape Flats. If you ever forget where you come from, if you ever lose sight of where you want to be, life will bring you home.

Navigating the Tension between Profit and Social Change

Jed Emerson, in Kickul and Lyons (2013), argues, "There is an idea that values are divided between the financial and the societal, but this is a fundamentally wrong way to view how we create value. Value is whole. The world is not divided into corporate bad guys and social heroes" (p. 148).

Pat Pillai has navigated the tension between profit and social change from the beginning. He does not regard himself as a social hero or as a corporate citizen. Instead, he approaches his enterprises with a holistic view of value that represents the intersection of money and meaning (Kickul & Lyons, 2013).

The traditional funding environment is being redefined by the collision of social gain that is often difficult to measure, with profit-maximising financial investment. And the stakes aren't small: it is estimated that $6 trillion in social-enterprises funding will be available by 2052 (Kickul & Lyons, 2013). Pat Pillai has intrinsically created an organisation with a hybrid structure that suits this shift in funding. LifeCo UnLtd is registered as both a for- and a not-for-profit, allowing the enterprise to access grant funding and risk-related capital that is more commonly associated with a startup than a charity.

This hybrid approach to funding social change differentiates social entrepreneurs from their commercial counterparts (Dees, 2001). Social entrepreneurs adopt a mission that creates and sustains social value, which requires constant innovation, adaptation and learning, with a deep sense of accountability to stakeholders and constituents (Dees, 2001).

As the model shows, Pat's approach is positioned in the middle of the funding spectrum. He has navigated the tensions of mission-driven profit, with his early focus on profit-driven strategies having disconnected him from the whims of the grant-funded environment.

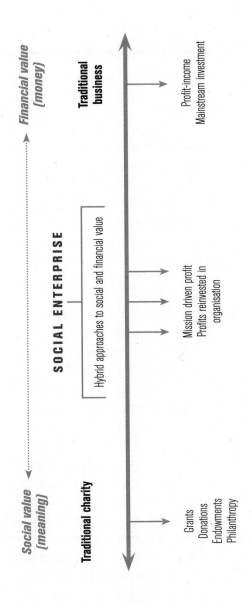

Social enterprise at the intersection of money and meaning

Adapted from Cheng, Goodall, Hodgkinson et al, 2010

GREGORY MAQOMA

THE MAN WHO DANCES FOR JOY

Turning his passion for the arts into a platform for building a business, Gregory Maqoma is moving hearts and minds to a bold new vision of social enterprise

The dancer leaps from shadow into light, his limbs rippling like water to the whip-sharp crackle of the drums. He catapults into the air, pushes against an invisible force, takes a slow, giant step, staggers backwards, spins, pirouettes, and stands, pointing into the void. The music stops. In the silence, a heartbeat, and then, loping at first, finding its feet, the music picks up the rhythm and commands the dancer to whirl and turn and spring, jackknifing his legs, framing his body with his arms. He is telling his story, in a language as old as the continent that gave him birth. The language of the heart, the language of the soul, the language of dance.

"Beautiful Me", he calls his story, and his name is Gregory Maqoma. His mother liked to tell him, when he was growing up in Orlando, Soweto, that he kicked before he was born, not like any other baby, but hard, and she thought, this boy is going to be a footballer. But already, there was a dancer in the family: Cecilia, his grandmother, who lived in Port Alfred in the Eastern Cape, and who did ballroom, with a grace and poise that left him breathless. He admired her as if she came from another planet, sent by the gods to teach him to dance.

"She was my first critic when I started taking dance formally," he says. "Change your posture, she would say to me, look out! But she was also my number-one fan." Today Gregory is the Executive Director and CEO of the Vuyani Dance Theatre in Johannesburg. The name, which is also his clan name, means joy. As a business enterprise, Vuyani is a curious hybrid between a commercial dance company and an NPO, staging dance productions for mainstream theatrical and corporate events, and running outreach programmes to train and develop the young dancers of tomorrow.

Beyond spreading a message of dance as a form of creative expression, the oldest and most universal of all human languages, Vuyani uses movement as an aid to understanding in the classroom. In a maths class, the dancers will use their hands and feet to form angles that cast new light on

geometry; in a science class, they will mimic the moods and energies of the four seasons, working in a lesson about the need to conserve and protect the environment. The curriculum, translated into choreography, leaps and twirls into life. Children learn the power of dance, and in holiday workshops, they learn to dance themselves.

Gregory is in the business of show, the business of razzle dazzle, as well as the business of making a social impact, reaching out to children, teaching them, showing them that dance can be a step up to a better life, just as it was for him. He dances between these worlds, and the balance keeps him on his toes. He sits in a classroom, a whiteboard behind him, the muffled sound of music and steps seeping through from the dancefloor next door. He is tall and limber, soft of voice, but he speaks in the vocabulary of dance, in the way he interlocks his fingers, and sweeps his arms in a gesture of embrace, and shrugs his shoulders and laughs.

Dancing is in his blood, but the truth is, he was never meant to make a living from it. He was a bright student, bright enough to earn a bursary to study medicine at the University of Cape Town. But his dream of being a doctor was deferred, because his parents couldn't afford to send him there. He listened to his calling. He had been listening to it all his life. In the 1980s, as a teenager, he fell in step with Michael Jackson, the King of Pop, mimicking his lunar footfalls, his pop-and-glide, the shuffle and the freeze, and the gloved hand on the brim of the hat. But he watched the migrant workers who lived near his home in Soweto too, taking note of their moves, their kicks and stomps that stirred up the dust.

The sting of teargas was in the air. Armoured vehicles were lumbering down the streets. South Africa was in a State of Emergency. In this cauldron of politics and heritage and popular culture, he fused emotion into motion, and the expression of it gave him joy. He formed a group with five of his friends: The Joy Dancers. They practised in backyards, and performed at weddings and school concerts. "It was a way," he says, "for us to escape the harsh reality in our township. Without knowing it, without even knowing what choreography was, we were already dealing with an aesthetic that was informing the future."

Dance is a concrete expression of abstract emotions. It is the spiritual, transformed into the physical. It is strict and precise in the mathematics of its movement, but it gives way to wild abandon, in the quest to achieve a state of grace. Anyone can dance. But not everyone can dance like Gregory Maqoma. He remembers his first audition, as a schoolboy, at the Moving into Dance studio in Braamfontein. He went with a friend from Soweto. "It was the first time we were entering a place where both black and white people were fighting for the same space, and the same opportunity," he says. "It was a frightening thing, because people were in tights, dance gear, which we hadn't seen. We thought we were in the wrong place. We had to convince ourselves that it was worth staying."

They passed the audition. The future his parents and schoolteachers had mapped out for him, his future as a doctor, drifted into the wind, and on that wind, he danced. If he has a gift, says Gregory, it is the gift of being able to recognise the gift in others. He wanted to be able to identify talent, and hone it and shape it and choreograph it. He wanted to build a company. In 1998, on a scholarship in Brussels, at the Performing Arts Research and Training Studios, he saw South Africa for the first time from the outside in, and he knew that he had to be a part of that changing landscape.

As part of a first-year project, he created a work called "Rhythm 1.2.3", a tribute and challenge to his home city of Johannesburg. He presented the work, which had already premiered at a dance festival in Amsterdam, and that marked the end of what was supposed to have been a three-year training course. "Listen," his teachers said, "we have absolutely nothing else to offer you. You are already an artist. You are already working. So go for your dreams. Go out there and explore."

The future his parents and schoolteachers had mapped out for him, his future as a doctor, drifted into the wind, and on that wind, he danced.

Back home, Gregory submitted a proposal for funding to the National Arts Council of South Africa, a statutory body set up to promote, through the arts, "the free expression of South Africa's cultures". Gregory had learned a bit about the free part. In Brussels, he had rehearsed his work for free at the school. Here too, for costumes, he had taken his pick from the racks at an Oxfam charity shop. For the set, he managed to get a pile of discarded cardboard boxes from a supermarket. He did the same back home in South Africa, where he performed the work with his fellow dancers, Shanell Winlock, Moya Micheal, and Zakhele Nkosi. The council rejected his proposal.

"I was absolutely beaten," says Gregory. "I thought, okay, how does one start a company without funding?" The arts are often the Cinderella child of public and private philanthropy in South Africa, but here, at the stroke of midnight, an outside party came to the ball. The Netherlands Embassy gave Gregory and his dancers a grant of R18,000, allowing them to stage their production, to great acclaim, under the banner of Vuyani. They were a company, born in joy, but only because there were three of them, and not because they had any notion of how a company should be run.

"We were doing everything ourselves," says Gregory. "We had no administration, nobody. Money would come into my personal account, and we would pay for this and this…we were negotiating everything. We didn't even pay taxes. We didn't know what tax was!" Financials, budgets, statements, expenses: these are not the natural beat for a company of dancers. But as the company grew, hiring dancers for funded productions, writing and submitting proposals, touring to raise more money, the business became a formality. In 2001, Vuyani registered as an NPO, dedicated to developing and mentoring promising young dancers, sending them back into their communities or accommodating them in the company.

Vuyani's Artistic Director, Luyanda Sidiya, for example, was mentored by Gregory for the position over the period of five years. "I want to see the chain," Gregory says. "I want to see an artist developing from the seed that has been planted. Someone who started very young, but because we took dancing to their school, they became really interested and chose dance as their career path. That genuinely is important." But the outreach programmes, with all their logistics, transport, and organisation requirements, were costing money, and money wasn't coming in. Within five years, Vuyani was a full-time dance company, a dozen strong, with an administrator and a management team and a steering committee, but no business model, and no marketing plan. They relied on goodwill and word of mouth, which can only go so far towards paying the bills.

"There were great and wonderful things we were doing," says Gregory, "but they were not income-generating. We were offering all these services for free. We were renting theatres to put on performances, and we were charging a minimum fee for tickets. If somebody called and said, I want to see the show but I don't have money, I said, come. We never closed any doors to anybody. So the income generated, compared to expenses, was not making sense." Even when the money did roll in, with a National Lottery grant of almost R1 million, it only added to the air of, don't worry, everything will be okay.

"We were never proactive," he says. "We were so relaxed. We had money, and it made us relax more." But every holiday comes to an end. In January 2008, after the Christmas break, Gregory had to tell his dancers there was no money left to pay them. We're trying hard, he said. Let's continue, and we'll see. He made a point of mentioning that he wasn't drawing a salary either. The next day, he walked into an empty studio. His dancers had quit.

He got a call from the director of a musical at the Sun City casino resort, about two hours' drive from Johannesburg. "I have seven or eight of your dancers here," he said. "Should I take them?" Take them all, said Gregory. He felt a sense of relief, and happiness for his dancers. They were working.

In the studio, on his own, he began dancing. Whirling, leaping, clutching at the air, his muscles as taut as the skin of a drum. He was alone. He commanded the space. He was free to explore his identity, to tell his story, with nobody watching. It was the stepping stone of his first solo work, and he called it "Beautiful Me". The company of his dreams, the company of joy, had been reduced to three musicians, two admin staff, and the dancer and choreographer, himself. But he had a work that was worth showing the world — engaging, masterful, mesmerising, said the reviews — and it was enough to keep the company alive. Some of the dancers came back to Vuyani, and the work evolved and grew to become "Beautiful Us". But amidst the joy and the beauty, ten years after its founding, the company still wasn't running as a serious business. It was still losing money.

> The company of his dreams, the company of joy, had been reduced to three musicians, two admin staff, and the dancer and choreographer, himself. But he had a work that was worth showing the world.

By chance, Gregory met Michelle Constant, arts journalist and CEO of Business and Arts South Africa, a public–private partnership between the corporate sector and the Department of Arts and Culture. "What is your board doing?" she asked. "Nothing. We don't even have meetings anymore," Gregory replied. "Wow," said Michelle, and that was the turning point, the pirouette, in the fortunes of Vuyani. Today the company has an active, involved board — two chartered accountants, a management consultant, a medical doctor with an MBA — and more than that, it has a strategy, a business model, a vision.

Gregory, who is a graduate in social entrepreneurship from GIBS, talks with ease about the diversification of income streams, the positioning of his brand, the strategy of reducing dependency on donors by at least 60 per cent. Vuyani works on contract for events companies, and Gregory is now his own word of mouth, knocking on the doors of major corporations to sell what he knows is more than a dance: it's a product, a service, a value-adding proposition.

"We are contributing to the creative economy," he says. "We are creating jobs with sustainability." There is merchandising, with calendars and DVDs. There is the festival circuit, and partnerships with dance companies in other countries. There is the outreach, the school holiday programmes, the collaboration with the maths academy next door. "We teach maths through movement. We show you the angles with your feet and hands."

You have to know all the angles, says Gregory. You have to think on your feet. You have to be hands-on. Every Monday morning, at the studio, he hosts what he calls a "check-in", a way of shaking off the dust and kick-starting the creation of a new week. "I might say, okay, I had this wonderful idea over the weekend. We look at it; how it can be done, how to strategise it. All these things get developed through teamwork, and the making of formulas. It has to get to a point where it is able to function smoothly without me."

The diary is packed. The jobs are rolling in, and they are generating money in turn. He talks of a production that went to Paris. It cost R300,000 to stage, and has already turned over three-and-a-half times that in revenue. He is looking at a space for Vuyani, a building to call its own. He wants the company to generate enough income to pay market-related salaries, but he worries, too, that it may become a victim of its own success. "At the moment as a dance company we are incredibly successful in the eyes of many people, including funders. Funders say, you guys are doing so well, why do you need money? You have to motivate. I think it boils down to how you communicate the strategy. I am not ashamed to say to a funder, I need money to make money."

He sees himself as a social entrepreneur, turning disadvantages into advantages, tackling a social problem and creating the financial value that can help to solve it. He is the Executive Director, the CEO, the strategist, the marketer. But still, it all comes down to that moment when the lights go down, when a hush falls over the audience, when the whip-crack of a drumbeat breaks the silence, and he moves from the shadow into the light, and he dances. This is his art, his passion, his business, his life, and this is why he does it. For the joy.

OPEN DANCE CLASSES

TUES	CONTEMPORARY/LATIN	17H30 – 18H30
WED	HIP HOP	17H30 – 18H30
THURS	AFRO RHYTHM	17H30 – 18H30
SAT	MODERN FUNK	09H30 – 10H30
SAT	YOGA	10H30 – 11H30

VUYANI
DANCE
THEATRE
0 1 9 - 4 6 5 - N P O

ANNUAL MEMBERSHIP FEE
R300.00

MEMBERS
R40.00 / SESSION
R300 / Month
NON-MEMBERS
R70.00 / SESSION
R400 / Month

1 President Street, The Dance Space building
Between Mariam Makeba & Henry Nxumalo Streets
Newtown 2113, Johannesburg, South Africa
Tel: +27 11 838-7666 Fax: 086 554 1244
E-mail: projects@vuyani.co.za
www.vuyani.co.za

MEMBERSHIP BENEFITS

Free classes upon first month of attendance

Eligibility for a discounted monthly subscription

Pay half-price per session

Eligible for discount tickets during VDT shows; and other related shows

NB: Membership is valid ONLY for 2015 non-refundable and non-transferable

Please note: We offer TEAM BUILDING WORKSHOPS at a reasonable price, call us for enquiries

A Transformation from Passion to Business

Gregory's story is one of learning over time through failure, restructuring, and resilience, and it is when he connects profit and reputation that he achieves sustainability. Dart, in Moizer and Tracey (2010), argues that NPOs must embrace commercial approaches in pro-business environments in order to be considered legitimate. Yet there is a risk in maximising both social and economic benefits because of the inherent tension that exists between the two approaches. Managing the "double bottom line" (p. 253) of resources and stakeholders is tricky and, if done poorly, threatens the sustainability of the organisation (Moizer & Tracey, 2010). What Gregory shows us is how reputation builds legitimacy, which acts as a glue between the two worlds.

Gregory contradicts the convention of the arts world as a grants-based, patronage-driven environment, and looks to profit as a means for both independence and creative input. His dancers spend time each week teaching in South Africa's townships, supporting maths and science, and this allows Gregory to identify raw talent and passion while inspiring young people. This is a creative example of Santos's (2012) description of social enterprises as organisations that create value.

Gregory's focus on profit and reputation has also brought structure, requiring an engaged board of trustees who hold him and his team accountable. The result of this is improved business efficiency, and consequently stability in line with Jiao's (2011) finding that connects business approaches and efficiency in NPOs. It is what Fury (2010) calls the "virtuous circle" (p. 1) of social entrepreneurship, that so deftly blends social and economic development with broad benefits to the organisation, and to the broader social context. Gregory's work is captured in a causal loop, where reputation creates the legitimacy that binds the opposite dimensions of impact and income, resulting in capital and social value.

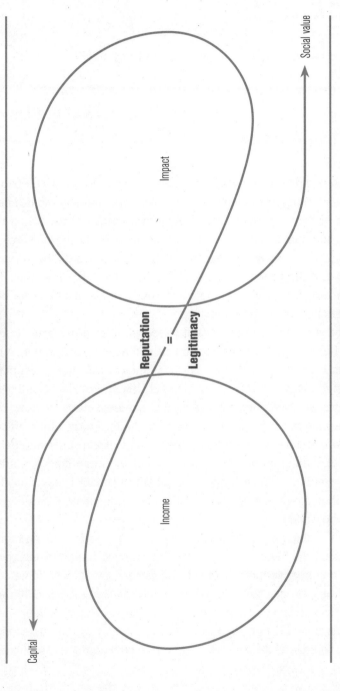

Reputation and legitimacy bind the opposite spheres of impact and income

Adapted from Molzer & Tracy, 2010

CLAIRE REID

THE BUSINESS THAT GREW IN A GARDEN

Sowing the seeds of enterprise and endeavour in a patch of backyard turf, Claire Reid has turned a school holiday activity into an invention that changes lives

A seed, carried on the wind, finds purchase on a patch of rocky ground. It lies in wait, exposed to the elements. The air stirs, marshalling its energies. A crack of lightning splits the sky. Rain falls, softly at first, driving the seed into the soil. It takes anchor, its roots questing and probing in search of nutrients. Nurtured, it grows strong, sprouting its way towards the surface, into the light, into the flowering of life. This is how plants are born. This, by the same process, is how ideas evolve, from swirls of thought into being. This is how thinkers become entrepreneurs.

Claire Reid is a planter of ideas, and more than that, a harvester. In the final year of her 20s, with wheat-blonde hair and a smile as bright as sunshine, she sits in the showroom of the business she has built from the ground up. She is the founder and CIO – Chief Impact Officer – of Reel Gardening, a company that produces herb and vegetable gardens, ready to grow. You can smell the sharpness, the salt of the earth, in the backroom of the offices in Blairgowrie, Johannesburg, where pinches of seed, sprinkled with organic fertiliser, are spaced and encased in strips of colour-coded tape. A garden on a ribbon, invented by Claire when she was still at school. It was a holiday activity, and then a science project, and then a social initiative, and then a sideline, and now, the roots of a fast-growing business.

You plant the strip above the soil, you water it daily, and in 40 days, give or take, you reap the harvest. Beans, beetroot, broccoli, butternut, cabbage, carrots, green pepper, lettuce, onions, peas, spinach, sweetcorn, tomatoes, basil, chilli, chives, coriander, marigold, nasturtium, parsley, rocket, sunflower. It is the most simple and down to earth of propositions. Nature is your silent partner. You do the hard work, and your reward is the joy of self-sustenance and food on the table. But Claire was not born to be a gardener. Her fingers are not green, she says.

As a child, she was always happier indoors. But she was born to be an entrepreneur, and curiosity and ambition would eventually lead her to venture

into other fields. She was seven years old, growing up in the suburb of Jukskei Park in Johannesburg when she started her first business. She made greeting cards with rubber stamps and ink pads, handing them out to family and friends on birthdays and other special occasions. Then she thought, everyone has a birthday. Everyone likes getting a card. A handmade card, especially. So she drew up a catalogue, printed it out, placed it in postboxes in her neighbourhood, and waited for orders. She would drop off the cards in a sandwich bag. Business was good. She was a bit older, but still at school, on her way back from swimming practice, when she saw two women fighting over a big black plastic garbage bin in the street.

Her father said, we need to get Claire to do stuff outside. He had the seed of an idea. If she would plant a vegetable garden, and tend it and nurture it and pick the crop, he would be her customer.

She turned to her mom and said, "Why don't they put their names on the bin? Then they'd know whose it is." Her mom wondered how you would do that without making it look messy. At home, Claire sprinted up the stairs and printed out the alphabet, in big, bold letters. She cut out the letters to make stencils, and charged people R20 to have their addresses spraypainted on their bins. You could see her handiwork all over the suburb. Every neatly labelled bin was a banner for her business.

She doesn't know where she gets it from, this instinct for ideas that blossom into enterprise. Her mother is a social worker, and her father is a quantity surveyor. "Neither of them have started their own business," she says. But they did instil in her a zeal for making things, for crafting items of value that people might want to purchase. She would do a lot of that, sitting in her room, toiling away with her hands, oblivious to the beckoning sun and the bright, pretty garden. She always knew that she was going to be an architect, and her gaze was drawn to interiors. One day, using the pocket money she had diligently set aside, she bought laminated-wood flooring, ripped up the carpet in her bedroom, and put the flooring down. "What kind of 16-year-old does that?" she asks. Her father said, we need to get Claire to do stuff outside. He had the seed of an idea. If she would plant a vegetable garden, and tend it and nurture it and pick the crop, he would be her customer. He would pay for the vegetables, the salad fresh from the earth, and he would provide the seed capital too. She didn't like the idea of gardening. But she liked the idea of business.

Up until then, if she needed capital goods – rubber stamps, ink pads, spraypaint – her parents would be her benevolent investors, her startup angels. But this was different. This was going to be a formal business arrangement. Her dad would loan her the money to buy what she needed from the garden centre, and she would pay him back from her profits. "I thought, whatever," she recalls. "How expensive can it be to start a vegetable garden?" At home, she measured a patch of turf, about three square metres, in the path of full sunlight, and she worked out what she could viably plant in it: six different varieties, about three to six seeds of each, because they needed space to breathe and grow. She took her list to the garden centre in Parktown North, and she picked out packets of seeds based on the prettiness of their pictures.

She held a packet of the tomato variety to her ear, shook it, and said to the sales assistant, "How many seeds are in here?" Oh, about four or five hundred, the assistant replied. "But I only want three!" said Claire. "Well, either you buy the full packet of seeds, or you don't. This is how seeds are sold." It was her first encounter, as a young professional, with the age-old enemy of creative thinking. The principle of Bureaucratic Intransigence, which says: this is the way we do things, because this is the way things have always been done. Claire couldn't understand why she had to spend R15 for a packet of 500 seeds, rather than, say, 30 cents for three seeds. But she had no option. She bought the packets, and then she needed fertiliser, which was only available in bags of one kilogram or more.

The whole exercise had already cost her R200 of borrowed money, and there was no way, she thought, that she was going to recoup that on fresh home-grown salads to order. "Claire," said her dad, "if you don't want to do it and you can't do it, that's fine." You do not say that sort of thing to Claire. It only spurs her on. She drew centimetre marks on her fingers, and got down on her knees in the vegetable garden, pushing holes in the moistened soil, and dipping the tiny seed in. But when she took her finger out, the seed was still on her finger.

"It was the most frustrating experience, to the point where I got up and walked away. I needed an extra pair of hands." Meggie was at home. Meggie Masilo, the family's domestic worker. The two of them sat at the vegetable patch, their hands dirty, shaking their heads. This was supposed to be simple work, good work, satisfying work. But it wasn't working. Claire would forget which seeds were which, and even when she did manage to get a few to stay in the ground, the hadedas, the squawking, dagger-beaked scavengers of the Joburg skies, would swoop in and peck them out.

Meggie told Claire how she had tried to grow a vegetable garden of her own, at her home in Rustenburg in the North West province. She couldn't read the English instructions on the single packet of seeds she had bought, and she had to make a roundtrip of nearly a kilometre to fetch water in a bucket. She planted in hope, and patted down the earth, and the weeds came, and strangled her crops. Claire, the suburban schoolgirl; Meggie, the rural villager. They both felt defeated, stupid, inadequate. *This is the way we do things, because this is the way things have always been done.*

No, thought Claire. She had learned how to work with her hands. She needed to find a way to regiment the seeds, to keep them in place, to feed and corral and grow them. Agriculture, the most ancient of human endeavours. In the garage, she found some old newspaper, and used it as a bed for the seeds. She made a paste from flour and water, the basis of papier mâché, and now the seeds had a bedrock. She anointed each seed with a droplet of SEAGRO, an organic fertiliser that made the kitchen smell of rotting fish. She had fashioned her prototype. A strip of seeds. A vegetable garden, ready to plant. Meggie took a strip with her to Rustenburg, and her friends wanted to buy. The ladies from the book club came to visit, and they wanted to buy. At first, Claire didn't understand: why couldn't they just make their own?

At school, where she was falling behind in science, her passport of entry for an architecture degree, her teacher told her she might be able to boost her marks by submitting a project for the Eskom Expo for Young Scientists. Claire demonstrated her invention. She called it Water-Wise Reel Gardening, because you could wind the strips on a reel, and plant them in a furrow, with the edge of the newspaper sticking up from the soil, like a banner. She ran tests on pH levels and irrigation. She concluded that you would use 80 per cent less water. She won the gold medal.

The Star ran a story, and Ronnie Kasrils, then-Minister of Water Affairs and Forestry, saw it. He phoned Claire. How would she like to represent South Africa at the Stockholm Junior Water Prize in Sweden? It was 2003. Claire was wearing her St Teresa's Mercy School uniform, and standing by her display. She was up against genius. The Korean student who had found a way to use bacteria to filter antibiotics from water. The German students who had engineered a fish tank that could power a computer, which in turn was programmed to feed the fish. She phoned home, in tears.

"Your product can make a difference in people's lives," her mother said. "You are there for a reason. You have something special. Genius lies in simplicity." The judges agreed. "An innovative, practical, easily applicable technique for planting and successfully germinating seeds in water-scarce areas to improve rural and peri-urban livelihoods," they wrote in their citation, awarding her the top prize. Simplicity became her mantra. Strip away everything that doesn't work and doesn't belong, until you have nothing left…but the strip. Plant it, nurture it, let it bloom. She was hoping, in the glow of her award, that someone would see the business potential of her invention, and grant her the capital to set the reels in motion. Instead, she got a government bursary to study for her Masters in architecture. She forgot about the gardening for a while.

In her practical year, between undergrad and postgrad, she spent a few days a month on a platinum mine in the North West, looking at ways of designing better houses for miners. The houses were tiny: 36 square metres. One way to improve them, she was told by the miners, would be to add a back door, so they wouldn't feel so boxed in. But when she spoke with the miners, there was one request that came up, over and over. "Why can't we have a little patch of ground to grow vegetables?" She saw that their lives were controlled by the punching of the clock, the descent of the cage into darkness and back into the light. The garden would give them quietude. A house would become a home. She took the idea to Anglo American, the owners of the mine, and they told her: "We tried that once before. It didn't work." They had handed out seeds and fertiliser. The miners had complained. Some had been given more seeds than others; some just didn't know or care how to grow vegetables from scratch.

> Simplicity became her mantra. Strip away everything that doesn't work and doesn't belong, until you have nothing left… but the strip. Plant it, nurture it, let it bloom.

"Well," said Claire, "what if you gave each miner a complete garden?" A seed had been planted. *Zimele*, Zulu for "to work", is the name of an enterprise-development initiative run by Anglo, to fund, support, and mentor small businesses. Suddenly, the architecture intern had an offer, in writing, that would turn her world upside down. A startup loan of R1 million, payable over 36 months, at five per cent, once her business started making money. She made the announcement over dinner at home. She was going to leave university, and set up Reel Gardening, for real. One million rand! Her parents were aghast. What if it didn't work? Who was going to stand surety for that much money? Claire had just one question: what's surety? The compromise, reached around a table at Anglo's head office, was that Claire would continue her Honours and Masters, and there wouldn't be surety – if the venture didn't work out, they would write off the loan.

Her parents thought it sounded too good to be true. At the same time, knowing Claire, they knew that it wasn't a gamble, and it was something more than a brazen vote of confidence. It was a dare. On 12 February 2010, from a converted dance studio fitted with desks made from old doors resting on top of boxes, Reel Gardening made its first sale. The client was Thrupps, an old-fashioned grocery store in Illovo, Johannesburg. They began stocking the seed-laden strips, which bore the legend, in terms of the contract: "Sponsored by Anglo American". *This is the way things have always been done. We tried that once before, and it didn't work.*

Now came another lesson in the hard science of running your own business. *Be careful what you wish for.* An order came in from Pick n Pay, the national supermarket chain, accompanied by a cheque for R100,000. They wanted Reel Gardening in 140 stores. It was like watching a time-lapse movie of a seed sprouting in seconds and bursting through the soil, too fast for its own good. This tiny company – back then it was just Claire, her boyfriend, Sean Blanckenberg, who had given up his job as a business consultant, and Catherine Corry, her project manager – was learning the hard way about demand and supply in the Big League of retail. The battle for shelf space, the pressure on margins, the 120-day payment cycle, the squeeze on cash flow, the rebates and advertising fees, the customers complaining that they couldn't find stock and then worse, when they found it, wanting to know: "Why am I buying this strip of seeds for R100, when I can buy a whole packet of seeds for R15?"

Claire had made the shift from backyard idea to entrepreneur, from school science expo to commercial marketplace, but people were not understanding the value of the proposition. "Each of our retail Gardens in a Box contains five different varieties of veggies as well as companion planting flowers," says Claire. "If someone wanted to buy this amount of variety in seed packets, they would have to buy eight packets of seed at R15 each, which would end up costing them R120. So they are actually saving money by not buying surplus that would just be wasted. It's always difficult to enter the market with a new product."

This may explain why retail sales now make up only four per cent of Reel Gardening's turnover. The rest comes from a mixture of training programmes, school gardens, Corporate Social Investment (CSI) partnerships, merchandising spinoffs, and joint ventures with big companies, such as Unilever. To promote their brand of curry spice called Rajah, Unilever wanted to encourage their customers to grow their own vegetables – onions, tomatoes, cabbages – to enjoy with their instant curry. So you buy the powder, and you get the box of seeds.

In time, with patience and care, you evolve from being a passive consumer to an active producer of goods. A farmer, in charge of your own little patch of turf. Claire, too, has evolved her enterprise, with the commercial products subsidising the provision of food gardens in schools and in water-scarce communities. Today, Reel Gardening is a Proprietary Limited (Pty Ltd) company, with a non-profit subsidiary called Reel Life, and ten employees, including Sean, who is now Director of Operations and Claire's husband. Anglo American's loan was repaid, the Pick n Pay contract came to an end, and the online store is thriving. Along the way, Claire has learned the big lesson: being an entrepreneur is lonely and tough, and nobody owes you a living. "You are not going to tap into some amazing pot of gold that the government has sitting there," she says. "You could enter a competition, like I did with the SAB Foundation Social Innovation Awards, and win R1 million. Anything is possible, but you cannot start a business banking on that."

You are the company, she says. Only you can make it work. "Unless you are extremely passionate about your product or service, and you really, really go to bed every night thinking, I did good today and I am happy – don't even start." But she is proof, too, that big things grow from small ideas, and that dreams, nurtured with sweat and toil, are scalable. To plant a seed, is to plant a garden.

The Shifting Roots of a Social Entrepreneur

Claire's story is one of innovation and scaling, from growing a science project into a business and then into a social enterprise. The evolution of her organisation starts with bricoleur-style entrepreneurship rooted in the communities and networks that she, Meggie and her parents are close to. The model shows how the agreements with Anglo American, and later with national retail chain Pick n Pay, turn Claire into a social-constructionist entrepreneur, where her focus becomes national, not requiring specific knowledge of a community, but rather of the broader market.

This precipitates an arms-length approach, distancing Claire from her former market, and requiring a more structured style with stakeholders, funders and commercial partners (Smith & Stevens, 2010). Smith and Stevens (2010) find that a wider geography of operation, with more distant relationships with stakeholders, forces the social entrepreneur to re-evaluate their social impact. Claire's markets are now further away, and so her agreements with partners are formalised and goal-oriented, with the commercial measure of sales being valued. This changes the rationale of her product and dilutes her social value. Claire does a U-turn on her scaling model, recognising that while scaling widely has expanded her market, it has not increased her impact. So she goes back to her bricoleur roots, setting up a not-for-profit that focuses on distribution to schools and rural communities, funded by the for-profit that is run not at arms-length, but from her offices, online and through specialist stores.

Claire's example shows that wider reach does not equate to increased impact. She has also had to make the difficult decision of profit over social mission, with the social mission proving central to the identity, culture and success of her business.

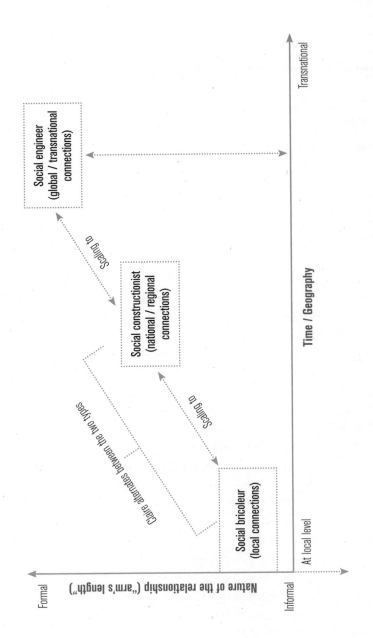

The nature of changing relationships for the social entrepreneur who scales

Adapted from Smith and Stevens, 2010

KOVIN NAIDOO

A MAN OF RADICAL VISION

Inspired by a chance meeting with a visionary of eyecare, Kovin Naidoo has combined the energy and idealism of an activist with the smart thinking of an entrepreneur, to build a public health institute that is changing lives and opening eyes

Vision is the primary sense, the impulse that gives light and shape and shade to the world around us. It is the sense that helps us to make sense of life: when we nod our heads and say, "I see," we mean, at last, that we understand. We get the picture. More than a gift, a blessing, a miracle that we take for granted, sight is a human right too. But for millions of people, says Professor Kovin Naidoo, optometrist, activist, CEO of the Brien Holden Vision Institute, a public health body and social enterprise that operates in 54 countries, it is a right restricted or denied by social circumstance. If you are too poor to afford an eye test and an appropriate pair of corrective spectacles, your vision may cloud, blur, fade into darkness. You will become a victim of refractive error, a flaw in the way light bends, or refracts, when it reaches the eye, leading to near-sightedness, farsightedness, astigmatism or presbyopia, a difficulty in focusing that is linked to ageing. And yet, at the end of this tunnel, there is light.

The institute, which works closely with governments and is funded mostly by the proceeds of commercialised research, has provided optometric services and glasses to over three million people at more than 400 vision centres and eyecare sites, and has trained more than 130,000 eyecare workers. But the numbers only begin to make sense, says Kovin, when you see a pair of eyes widen behind a pair of glasses, as light comes flooding in and the world shifts brightly into focus. The other day, he visited a vision centre in a rural village in Malawi. "You see these people who have never had access and then you ask them, what do you want to read? And they say, I want to read the Bible. You can talk about careers and all of that, but these are the simple things, and they are important. I am not religious, but at the end of the day, that is the centre of their world."

As a social enterprise, the Brien Holden Vision Institute runs on a unique template of public and private collaboration, linking clinics, hospitals, practitioners, educators, researchers and suppliers in a chain of value that makes

eyecare accessible and affordable to all. But that's just a start. According to a study by the institute, all it would take to prevent blindness or vision impairment caused by refractive error, is a once-off global investment of $28 billion. That in turn would save $202 billion a year in productivity lost due to avoidable eyecare problems. A long-term, sustainable solution to a major public-health challenge.

This is not a dream. It is a vision. It begins at the intersection of cultures and continents, with a meeting of minds that would change lives and open eyes. At the time, Kovin was a Senior Lecturer of Optometry at the University of Durban-Westville, which would later become part of the University of KwaZulu-Natal. He had an urge to "go some place I had not seen before"; it was almost as if he had jabbed his finger at a spinning globe, and it had led him to South Korea, for the World Optometry Conference in 1997.

Kovin, now almost 50, is a man of quiet fire, forged during his tenure as a student leader during the struggle against apartheid. And here he had come to present something radical, born from his conviction that optometry has a duty to correct social ills, to help ward off the loss of hope and opportunity that is a needless consequence of diminishing vision. His paper proposed a visionary new model of training and deployment for optometry students, recalibrating the focus from private to public healthcare in developing nations. He called it the Multiple Entry and Exit Model. In essence, he was saying that optometry students shouldn't need to have waited until they were fully qualified before they could work in the field. Instead of training to degree level, they could earn modular credits and gain experience at varying levels of clinical expertise, before returning to continue their studies. After first year, for instance, a student with basic skills would have learned enough to work as an eyecare screener or educator at a community clinic. They could dispense reading glasses, screen for refractive conditions, and refer patients for further treatment. A year later, the student could qualify as a dispensing optician and lab technician, finally moving into diagnostic and therapeutic practice after an accumulative four years of training. This staggered approach, designed to address a glaring lack of eyecare personnel and facilities in Africa, was bound to be contentious, conceded Kovin. He was right.

"A lot of people in the audience said to me, you are trying to destroy our profession by training lesser-trained people. Our business will suffer. They were only thinking about the private sector. They didn't see the value in the public sector. I was a bit disappointed. Your first major conference, and afterwards the audience want to lynch you. It is not a nice feeling." But the next day, Kovin found a kindred spirit, in the form of an Australian academic and contact lens practitioner, who took to the podium to say, "As Naidoo said, if we don't do something, this profession will become obsolete on the continent of Africa." His name was Professor Brien Holden. A burly, impassioned man with a Colonel Sanders-style goatee, he was celebrated in his homeland as a scientist with an entrepreneurial streak, capable of translating laboratory research into commercially viable products. One of his big breakthroughs, as team leader, was the formulation of silicone hydrogel contact lenses, which allow wearers to sleep comfortably at night, and are also used in products to slow myopia in children. In part, the royalties from such innovations help to fund humanitarian programmes, bringing quality eyecare and treatment to impoverished communities. It was here that Brien saw eye to eye with Kovin, over dinner at the conference that night.

"Brien was trying to promote contact lenses across the world," recalls Kovin. "He started realising around that time that this is difficult. You cannot promote contact lenses to people who don't have running water. He learned through that process that access to eyecare was the real issue. He said we should work together. I said fine." Back to their separate continents they went, their common interest bridged by an NGO called the International Centre for Eyecare Education (ICEE). Its mission was clear: "To help eliminate avoidable blindness and impaired vision, particularly due to uncorrected refractive error." The idea was that Brien would run the global organisation, as an addendum to his income-generating research and development, while Kovin would set up an African subsidiary as an independent trust. It would be a partnership, a social franchise, with Brien acting as a mentor and funder as well.

He already had a reputation as a skilful organiser, quick on his feet, a rouser of hearts and minds, going all the way back to his schooldays in the township of Chatsworth, near Durban.

Initially, Kovin wanted to set the trust up through the university, but he was dissuaded by the rector, Professor Mapule Ramashala, who said, "Kovin, you move too fast. The university processes will kill you." She was right, he admits. "She saw the value in having something associated with the university expanding rapidly, but if we had registered through the university, if I wanted a pen, I would have had to requisition one. My mind works too fast for that. I am impatient about getting things done. I want it done now." He already had a reputation as a skilful organiser, quick on his feet, a rouser of hearts and minds, going all the way back to his schooldays in the township of Chatsworth, near Durban.

At 14, together with his older brother, Kumi, he led a boycott of classes that got the two of them expelled. They told their father, Shunmugam, a bookkeeper, that they had been forced to take part in the boycotts, or risk being branded as sell-outs. But their bluff was called when the principal phoned and said, "Come and get your boys, they're causing trouble." They were allowed to write exams, and returned to school after a successful court case against the Minister of Education. It was a time of turmoil for the boys, whose mother, Mana, had died tragically just before the boycotts began. Kovin credits her for his sense of social justice. "The neighbours and the people around us were generally working class and poor," he says. "My mom was very good at making sure we were sensitive to the social conditions. She was not political, but religious. Religious in a sense that she always felt that you live your life and express your faith through your actions. I think it rubbed off."

During his months in solitary confinement, Kovin had often wondered, what happens when the Struggle is over? What will I do with my life? Now he knew. He wanted to go back home.

The two brothers were fervent social and community activists, raising money for feeding schemes and drought relief, and starting an athletics club in their neighbourhood. But they had bigger ambitions. "We were at school, remember," says Kovin. "We were trying to draw kids into our movement, Helping Hands, through other means. Once they got in, it was a chance for us to influence them, and many of them became political activists, and have gone on to make a big contribution. We learned a lot about organising, about how you adapt to communities, rather than having this attitude of, I know the answer so I will come and tell you how to do things. We had to learn all the time."

They learned their lessons well. Kumi went on to study politics in London, and would later become CEO of the global environmental NGO, Greenpeace. Kovin graduated with a BSc at the University of Durban-Westville. He wanted to go on to study medicine, but his peers had other plans for him. He was President of the Students' Representative Council, and in 1988, during a nationwide State of Emergency, he had been detained in solitary confinement for eight months. He completed part of his studies by the dim light of a jail cell, struggling to concentrate after hours of daily interrogation. Following the transition to democracy, he had hoped to continue his studies at the medical school of the University of the Witwatersrand, as there was no medical school at Durban-Westville at the time. "But the activists met and decided I couldn't leave campus because of the role I was playing. They said, we have followed you as a leader, and now the time has come for the collective to decide what you should do," says Kovin. "I sat in a meeting where even first-year students were involved in the discussion, and I was told that I was not allowed to comment. They discussed what I should do. The decision was that I couldn't leave the university. So that is how I ended up in optometry."

He struggled at first with his coursework, in part because optometry was virgin territory for a seasoned political activist. There was very little leadership or lobbying around public health in the profession, which had a reputation as a more lucrative discipline than general medicine. In his first-year lectures, he kept getting told how much money he was going to make. "They never spoke about the fact that 80 to 90 per cent of people don't have access. It was very frustrating for me." But in that gap, Kovin found his calling. "It was the best decision somebody else took for me," he says. "My colleagues gave me the career I could not have imagined. Sometimes, as my grandmother said, things work out for a reason."

After graduating, he decided to study further in public health. With a Fulbright Scholarship, he signed up for a concurrent Doctor of Optometry at the Pennsylvania College of Optometry, and a Masters in Public Health at Temple University. "I did one during the day and one at night," he says. "Two different universities. They were 15 minutes from each other by train. I would finish one, get on a train, do another trip there, and come back. I just got it out of the way." During his months in solitary confinement, Kovin had often wondered, what happens when the Struggle is over? What will I do with my life? Now he knew. He wanted to go back home.

In Durban, he took up a teaching position at his alma mater, but it wasn't long before he realised how little had really changed after liberation. A graduate approached him, hoping Kovin could help in his search for a job in optometry. "I said to him, how can you need a job? You are the only practitioner in a black township that desperately needs service. Did you buy a BMW? No. Did you buy a house? No. Did you buy gifts for girlfriends or whatever? Okay, I said, bring your financials." Having a degree, it turned out, wasn't enough. Without a network, without connections, the young graduate was struggling to set up his practice. Kovin did what came instinctively to him as a former student organiser. He called a meeting.

From that was born Clear Vision, a co-operative of optometrists that grew to encompass 143 practices. "We ended up with the best discount structure in the country," says Kovin. "We started negotiating with the big labs and the big groups. We had a fair amount of companies that were saying, look, the country is changing, we want to work with you. When we reached a level where we couldn't grow it any more, I said to the practitioners, this is a good opportunity for you. If you want to take it to the next level, you will need to merge with one of the big groups." That turned out to be Spec-Savers, a leading South African optometry chain, who acquired Clear Vision and gave the practitioners shares in the company. Kovin, who had no interest in entering full-time private practice, accepted a seat on the board of the holding company, Spec-Savers SA.

"Even though I wasn't involved on a daily basis," he says, "I learned a lot about business. I realised that even business is about organising, it is about people and organising. Of course you learn something about being able to read balance sheets and so on. I had done accounting at high school, and it wasn't rocket science. Read the information, and start using the terms as if you know what you are talking about. It is not difficult." He learned, too, of the curious imbalance in the economics of optometry, with 80 per cent of practitioners chasing 20 per cent of the market. The real value, as always, lay at the bottom of the pyramid. The deal proved Kovin's capabilities as an activist, lobbyist, negotiator and entrepreneur, but the big test would be the establishment and running of the Africa-based institute that sprang from that dinner with Brien Holden in South Korea.

With funding from the commercialisation of Brien's research, Kovin bought a house to accommodate trainees, close to the university campus in Durban. To run it, he tracked down a beloved figure from his childhood. Philisiwe Mathonsi, the domestic worker who had raised him after the death of his mother. "I knew how she cooked, I knew how nice she is to people," says Kovin. "She is very motherly. I recommended her to the organisation and she started working for us. It was great. She had a job, and she wasn't a domestic worker any longer."

The priority for ICEE Africa was education: to find and train eyecare workers who could go on to train other workers in basic optometry. That immediately brought Kovin into conflict with the optometric establishment. "The attitude was, why are you training nurses? That is our job. I said, maybe it is your job, but you are not doing anything. What must we do, go to government and say, wait 50 years until optometry grows on the continent? I would sit at South African Optometric Association conferences and speakers would give an address, and say, 'Some people think…' And that somebody was me, and I would be attacked. I thought I was doing the right thing. There were some really lonely times around this thing." But the training went on, with trainee ophthalmic nurses coming from across Africa, learning how to conduct eye exams and fit glasses, and being dispatched back home to work in the field.

But the bigger issue was the glasses themselves. At the time, the average price was R600 a pair, well beyond the reach of an NGO with a public-health mission. Once again, for Kovin, the answer lay close to home.

"I had a neighbour from Chatsworth who was very entrepreneurial," he says. "He grew up with not much, like all of us, but ended up becoming a multimillionaire by working really hard. Really honest, great guy. He had set up offices in China. I spoke to him and said, I need your help." Kovin travelled to China with him, visiting factories, making sure no child labour was involved, negotiating hard for discounts on frames and lenses. "I remember this one guy was being translated. I was talking and he was looking at me. I said, I think you understand, can I talk to you directly? He said, okay. I said, me, I work with poor people. I need you to help me. He said, I understand, special price. That was all he said, then he went from $3 to $1. He said, we won't compromise on the quality." That was a hefty drop from the original quote of $80 for a pair of glasses, and it allowed Kovin to set up a Global Resource Centre to supply his projects and make eyecare affordable to all. The centre was able to make a small profit from the sale of glasses, helping to sustain clinics, pay staff, and cross-subsidise other eyecare treatments. "We began using a social enterprise strategy of generating income," says Kovin. "Government didn't have to pay for our services."

With the income supplemented by donor funding for the training and employment of optometrists, ICEE, since renamed the Brien Holden Vision Institute in honour of Brien's groundbreaking work, has been able to set up vision centres across Africa and as far afield as Cambodia, Vietnam, Pakistan, and the Middle East. Today, with a chain of value that incorporates education, eyecare, research and commercialisation, Kovin has developed a model of social business that sits somewhere between an NGO and a private enterprise. Social entrepreneurship, he says, has allowed him to break away from the old binaries. "You were either a communist or a capitalist," he says. "You had to choose which side you were on. In that sense, it is very exciting to be in a space that can be defined by values rather than ideology. That can be risky if you go into it thinking you know all the answers. But the people who have been successful are those who have gone in and said, well there isn't

Social entrepreneurship, he says, has allowed him to break away from the old binaries. "You were either a communist or a capitalist...You had to choose which side you were on. In that sense, it is very exciting to be in a space that can be defined by values rather than ideology."

just one model that I will adopt."

Kovin likes to think big, beyond the boundaries that divide one way of doing business from another. He calls it the Seven Billion Model. There is a pyramid, and at the base is the public sector, run by governments, and often supported by NGOs. Higher up is the private sector, and between them, the social entrepreneurship and social franchise space. Social entrepreneurship is epitomised by the vision centres that generate a small income, and the social franchises, run by small entrepreneurs in underserved areas, with the primary aim of creating access. This space is also supported by some in the private sector, where optometrists can offer affordable packages, using frames and lenses that are usually supplied by NGOs and subsidised programmes. "The more people get taken out of the government sector, the more people get taken out of the NGO sector, the better it is," says Kovin. "If people have money and the private sector can serve them, why not? There are seven billion people. The market is big enough. Why would we want to keep investing and setting up new things, if the private sector can care for some of them? The poorest of the poor will then have more resources available for them when they access the public sector."

Either way, it all comes down to that moment when a new pair of glasses is fitted, and someone, young or old, sees the world in a whole new light. Sadly, in July 2015, Brien Holden, the visionary who started it all, died suddenly, at the age of 73. But through Kovin and the institute, his work lives on, and so, with every flicker of light, does his vision.

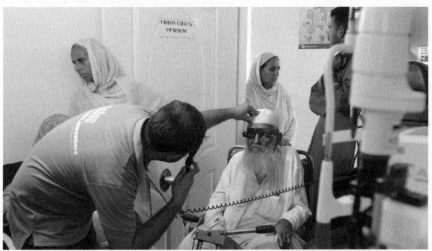

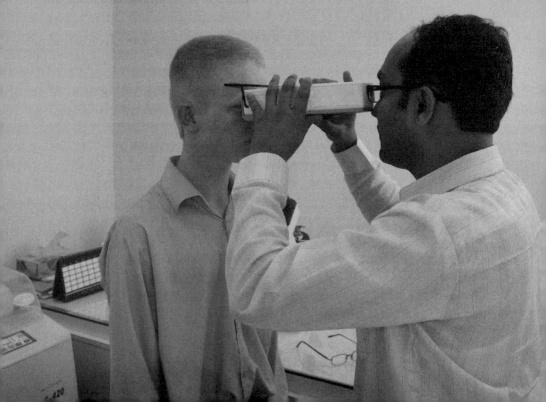

How Franchising Reimagines the Social Enterprise

Social franchising applies commercial principles of franchising to achieve social goals. It is particularly suited to accessible private healthcare services in developing and middle-income countries, where there is a preference for private healthcare irrespective of income (Thurston, Chakraborty, Hayes, Mackay & Moon, 2015). Private healthcare, with faster and better customer care, is regarded as being more accessible than public healthcare. It is a model that enables quality assurance through a network of independent healthcare, with the franchisor providing training, mentoring, and support, while the franchisee delivers services within the quality standard framework (Thurston et al., 2015).

South Africa's public health service struggles to provide a comprehensive, quality service. The country consistently ranks in the lower end of health indices in the Global Competitiveness Report[1] (Schwab, Sala-i-Martin, Eide, & Blanke, 2014; World Health Organization, 2015).

Kovin has responded to the country's poor healthcare by setting up ICEE/Brien Holden Vision Institute to provide accessible eyecare to people in underserved markets. His Seven Billion Model sees opportunity in the *systemic space* between government, civil society organisations, and the private sector, which has enabled him to scale successfully to 54 countries. Scaling is a complex process for social enterprises, and particularly for social franchises, as the franchisee is not an individual, but an organisation (Lyon & Fernandez, 2012). Thurston et al. (2015) identify enablers that influence the successful scaling of social franchises in healthcare. Firstly, there needs to be institutional capacity in the private healthcare sector, and an underserved group who seeks, and is prepared to pay for, services from private health providers. This commonly occurs in environments where the public healthcare sector cannot meet needs, but the government is not averse to partnering with the private sector, recognising the need for the provision of services.

---

1 The Global Competitiveness Report ranks a country's performance against established criteria out of a total of 144 countries. South Africa ranks 143rd in terms of tuberculosis infections per 100,000 citizens. The country ranks 140th for HIV prevalence as a percentage of the adult population. It is ranked 129th for life expectancy, and 136th in terms of the business impact of HIV/Aids and tuberculosis.

There is also an enabling policy environment, which supports task sharing, so that mid-level providers can supply franchised services. Finally, Thurston et al. (2015) find that there are resources available for the franchise and management structures to be set up.

Kovin's approach to scaling integrates these enablers. He uses the institutional environment, recognising the systemic gaps that exist, and sets up a trainee network that builds capacity and ensures quality across a network. In China, his negotiation secures low-cost, high-volume orders that don't compromise on product quality. He operates in a hybrid environment, reliant on co-funding from the patents of the Brien Holden Vision Institute, while operating in countries where governments are willing to partner with service providers, and where policy is supportive of the scaling of social franchises. His Seven Billion Model reimagines the typical cyclical model that interlinks business, government and civil society, as a hierarchy that reveals systemic gaps and opportunities for social enterprises.

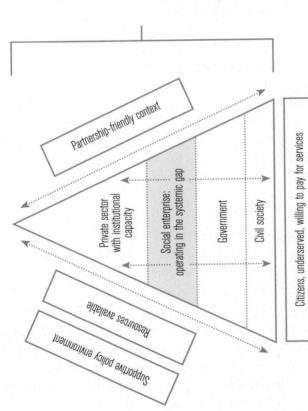

KOVIN'S RESPONSE

- Identifies system gaps
- Builds hybrid organisation to respond across sectors
- Identifies policy-friendly environments
- Develops alternative models of financing social value

SOCIAL FRANCHISING ENABLERS

1. Institutional health capacity in private sector
2. Underserved groups requiring private healthcare
3. Overburdened public healthcare unable to meet demand
4. Government not averse to partnering with private sector
5. Customers and third parties willing to pay for services
6. Adequate resources for social franchise setup
7. Environment not averse to task sharing

Partnership-friendly context

Private sector with institutional capacity

Social enterprise: operating in the systemic gap

Government

Civil society

Supportive policy environment

Resources available

Citizens, underserved, willing to pay for services

Social franchising enablers applied to Kovin's Seven Billion Model

Adapted from Thurston et al, 2015

TADDY BLECHER

AN ALCHEMIST OF HUMAN POTENTIAL

Packed and ready to leave for an international career, Taddy Blecher changed his mind and stayed in South Africa, to build institutes of free tertiary learning that have helped to unlock the prospect of greatness in even the poorest of communities

Little Taddy Blecher looked up at the stars, his head reeling at the dizzying infinity of the cosmos. He was out in the country, where the air is pure and the sky is deep, dark, and clear. In the great blazing trail of the Milky Way, he learned the names of stars and traced the shapes of constellations. He saw the stars as his friends. Then, one night, back in the big city, he ran outside and looked up. But all he saw was a grey haze, a veil that divided him from the faraway worlds of his dreams. His friends, overnight, had disappeared. He ran in to lodge a formal complaint with his mother. It is one of Taddy's earliest memories, a glimmer of what was to become his life's quest: to find the trailblazers, the brightest stars, and set them free to shine. That haze, many years later, would lift to reveal the two institutes of learning that have allowed him to test a thesis that is celestial in its ambition. "Every human being," says Taddy, founder of CIDA City Campus and the Maharishi Institute, "is made of genius."

Even a child from the poorest of backgrounds, living in the most unequal society in the world – South Africa, according to a World Bank survey in 2014 – can be moulded and shaped into a graduate, an entrepreneur, a business leader. In this view of the world, the Gini coefficient, a measure of the distribution of income in a country, is seen not as a prophecy of doom, but as a hurdle, waiting to be overcome. That's why we call it the human race. When Taddy went to university, to study actuarial science, he was struck by the harsh reality of economic theory, the cold Darwinism at its heart. In the battle for scarce resources, you either win or you lose. And if you come from a background of relative wealth, comfort and privilege, as Taddy does, well, you are a lot more likely to win. But he detected a flaw in the theory.

"Human beings are alchemists," he says. "We have an infinite capacity to turn potential into opportunity." And the tool that we use, the hammer that taps lead into gold, is education. Before we explore what that means, let us

quickly resolve a lesser, yet nagging, mystery. Why is Adam Paul Blecher, actuary, activist, social entrepreneur, pioneer of free tertiary education in South Africa, better known to everyone by his childhood nickname, Taddy? The answer comes via his mother, Leonae. "When I was pregnant with Tad," she says, "his father, Dr John Blecher, who was a gynaecologist, would come in from his rooms in the Park Lane Clinic and say, 'How are you, and how's the tadpole?' The tadpole being the Taddy-in-utero. After he was born, the closest name we could find to 'tadpole' was Adam Paul. But everyone has always called him Taddy."

To meet the tadpole today, in the offices of the Maharishi Institute, a non-profit business and life-skills college in Marshalltown, Johannesburg, is to see that starry-eyed wonder, un-dimmed, magnified behind the rimless spectacles that frame his boyish face. He has a shock of jet-black hair, and eyebrows that seem to have a life of their own, raised in curiosity, dipped in quick, quizzical contemplation. He is a generous listener, leaning in to grasp a point and hold it up to the light, and as a talker, he is restless and expansive, using his hands with the expressiveness of a conductor on a podium. He is talking about poverty, and the most effec-tive way to get rid of it. By degrees. "In South Africa, 96 per cent of people with a degree are employed," he says. "So if you want to get rid of poverty quickly, in one generation, put people through a degree."

> "In South Africa, 96 per cent of people with a degree are employed. So if you want to get rid of poverty quickly, in one generation, put people through a degree."

A degree equips you with marketable skills and know-how, but more than that, it teaches you how to think. And herein lies a para-dox. The deep source of Taddy's energy, his alertness, is his ability to shut out the noise of the world, to turn his mind inward and think of nothing, for at least 20 minutes twice a day. To meditate, transcendentally. The Maharishi Institute is housed in an austere nine-storey block on Ntemi Piliso Street, just across the road from the Johannesburg Magistrate's Court. It has the look of raw, unfinished concrete. But the real building material lies within. Here, students come from townships, informal settlements, and rural villages across the country, their tuition fees paid largely by grants and donor funding. Their coursework is a four-year Bachelor of Business Administration (BBA) degree, accredited by the Maharishi University of Management in the USA and the Regenesys Business School, and integrated with the teachings of the Indian guru from whom the institute takes its name.

Maharishi Mahesh Yogi, famous in the 1960s as the spiritual adviser to

The Beatles, developed the practice of TM, or Transcendental Meditation, which claims to reduce stress and enhance creativity, intelligence, and learning ability. At the institute, it's an everyday part of the "consciousness-based" curriculum, along with early morning yoga sessions. Does it work? For Taddy, the proof is in the people. He tells the story of a group of 20 Maharishi graduates who were interviewed for a graduate programme run by Accenture, the strategic-consulting company. "The guy who did the final interviews phoned me the next day," says Taddy, "and he said, 'I want to tell you, I got home at 4 am and spent an hour and a half writing a letter to the whole leadership of Accenture in South Africa, to tell them that I think we should start almost exclusively recruiting from you, because of the quality of the people you are producing.'" He said he had never seen such well-rounded candidates. In the end, Accenture took 17 of the 20 Maharishi graduates into its programme, among them a 35-year-old man, born into poverty, who had previously worked as a gardener. As you sow, so shall you reap.

It is part of the academic tradition at the institute that graduates, once they find employment, contribute towards the tuition costs of a student who follows in their footsteps. This principle of pay it forward is combined with a programme called Learn and Earn, which sees students working in a customised call centre on campus. They gain valuable work experience, and their earnings are ploughed back into the running of the institute. There is outreach too: the students go back to their home communities during holidays, to share their experiences and run short courses on mathematics, financial literacy, computer skills, and healthy living. The goal is not just to transfer learning and recruit the next intake of matriculants. It is also to create a radical model of tertiary education that funds, supports, and sustains itself, with no need, ultimately, for government subsidies or corporate donations. A university of knowledge in perpetual motion, where students earn to learn, as they learn to earn.

In a country where university students took to the streets to demand affordable education, as part of the #FeesMustFall protests of 2015, this may sound like a utopian vision. But for Taddy, it is a practical plan of action, and it begins, as everything does, with constructive meditation on the challenge at hand. "The model of education has to change in the world, because it is too expensive and too elitist," he says. "Places like Harvard build an elite network, and then the network becomes the intelligentsia, and they build great businesses. Harvard works because you are taking the cream of the crop. But what if you are taking the failures of the crop? Can you produce Harvard quality, and even better? That is what we are really interested in.

Can you take a street kid and turn him into a merchant banker?" But Taddy is an actuary by training, and he doesn't dream, he projects.

Since the establishment of the Community and Individual Development Association (CIDA), the founding organisation of both CIDA City Campus and the Maharishi Institute, of which Taddy is the CEO, more than 14,250 young people have been impacted by the work of the organisation, about a third of them as entrepreneurs. "Very conservatively," says Taddy, "we believe that all of these people will earn upwards of R17 billion in combined salaries in their working careers. Based on surveys we have done, they are breadwinners now for over 70,000 people. If we can meet our target of putting a hundred thousand people through degrees, we estimate that they will earn over half-a-trillion rand in the course of their careers. That is huge change."

> He was struck not just by the poverty and squalor, but by the sharp contrast to his own comfortable life, packed with opportunity and possibility, symbolised by the 43 boxes… that were lined up at home for his relocation to the USA.

But there is another question begging here, and it is this: why would a man with one of the most sought-after professional qualifications in the world, a degree in actuarial science, abandon his plans to live and work abroad, and devote himself instead to a social cause that is generally thought to be the province of government departments and philanthropists?

Every story of social entrepreneurship has its turning point, its moment of epiphany and revelation, and for Taddy, it was a visit to a black township in 1995, in the rainbow-hued afterglow of South Africa's transition to democracy. He was struck not just by the poverty and squalor, but by the sharp contrast to his own comfortable life, packed with opportunity and possibility, symbolised by the 43 boxes – an actuary always keeps count – that were lined up at home for his relocation to the USA, and a prize job as a strategic consultant for the Monitor Group in Boston. Leaving, he thought, lying wide awake in bed that night, would be the coward's way out. All things being unequal, he felt a duty, a compulsion, to try and fix a system that had been counterweighted to benefit him, as a white South African, all his life. His first impulse was to open his wallet, but all that did was lighten his conscience. The answer was: get down to work.

"Just having a good heart and wanting to make a difference isn't enough," says Taddy. "But if you pick any area and you put your heart and soul into that, you can fundamentally change the system." He picked education, in part because he saw himself as proof of concept. At school, he had been a slow, unfocused learner, until his brother taught him the techniques of Transcendental Meditation that would become a habit for life. He joined CIDA, an NPO that ran schools and teaching projects across the country. Taddy taught TM to matric students in Soweto and Alexandra, helping them to sharpen their concentration and improve their marks, but what was there beyond that? What were the chances of them being able to afford a quality tertiary education? The country had been liberated from apartheid, with its vision of black workers as "hewers of wood and drawers of water", but just how free would the new generation be from that age-old destiny?

Just five years down the line from that train of thought, Taddy was standing in front of a class at the CIDA City Campus in downtown Johannesburg, in an old building that had previously housed a teachers' training college. It was 2000, and the first free university in South Africa was open for business, with 250 students and no computers. Taddy handed out photocopies of a computer keyboard to his class, and he put a song by Bob Marley on the stereo. He showed them how to type along to its slow, hymnal rhythm. "Emancipate yourselves from mental slavery, none but ourselves can free our minds." A song of redemption had been born. CIDA grew from the seed of an ideal – free tertiary education for poor South Africans – into a model of a sustainable social enterprise that attracted support and attention from across the globe. The individual donors included the American talkshow host, Oprah Winfrey, and the serial entrepreneur, Sir Richard Branson, and the money was channelled through an empowerment fund that was worth about R200 million in its heyday.

For Taddy, the key to the success of CIDA was its "nuts and bolts" business approach to fixing tertiary education. Donor companies would draw from the pool of graduates, for instance, and in one model of quid pro quo, a banking group employed students as paid interns, sending them into the field to market the bank's services in their own communities. Everybody learns, everybody earns, everybody wins. "Tons and tons of social enterprises and charities fail in South Africa," says Taddy. "Especially now in the 21st Century, charity is dead. This is the age of the social entrepreneur, and if it's a non-profit or for-profit model, it doesn't matter, it has to be killer competitive, it has to be in the 21st Century and it has to stand on its own two feet. It cannot be a begging bowl and survive." The irony is that CIDA City Campus got the business model right, but it collapsed anyway, a victim of colliding visions and ideologies around the boardroom table.

Taddy was the CEO, and he calls the conflict, which led to the deregistration and eventual liquidation of the campus in 2015, "probably the saddest moment of my life". Taddy saw the campus as a place of holistic learning, with Transcendental Meditation as a core component of the curriculum. Other board members felt differently. "Everything we believed in – developing human potential, students engaging in the community, everything that was not just the academic – was going to be removed out of the organisation," says Taddy. "We said, look, this is such a beautiful organisation and we believe you are going to destroy it if you go down that path. And rather than watch it being destroyed, we will leave with nothing. You can have everything, and we will go and build other free universities, because South Africa needs as many free universities as we can create."

That meant leaving behind the empowerment fund, a downtown Johannesburg property portfolio worth R100 million, a painstakingly established global brand, and a coalition of high-profile corporate and individual donors. "We agreed that we would not take a single donor away," says Taddy. "We started again from scratch. That is the hardest thing. If you are going to use donor funding, the reality is that donors have their own minds, and you might lose your donors if you don't do what they want. But if you just do what they want, you might never do anything great. It is tough, very tough." Based on the same model as CIDA City Campus, the Maharishi Institute is currently 50 per cent self-funded, and its donors include such big names as the Rockefeller Foundation, the Oppenheimer family, Roche Pharmaceuticals, Sasol, Microsoft, and Cisco.

Every year, the new graduates, now rich with knowledge and know-how, go out into the workplace, and the counter keeps clicking on that big dream target of 100,000 tertiary degrees and half-a-trillion rand in lifetime earnings. But still, if you ask Taddy what he considers to be his own greatest achievement, as an activist and social entrepreneur, he doesn't waste any time mulling over it. "I still feel like a failure," he says. "I still feel we haven't scratched the surface of what we want to do." He thinks of Oxford and Cambridge and Harvard, and the way they built institutions, cities, ecosystems of learning in the middle of nowhere, to send wave after wave of enlightenment into the world. Why can't we do that over here? Is it because South Africa is a second-class nation? He shakes his head in answer to his own question. We are all made of genius.

"A lot of people say to us, well if you haven't had early childhood development, you are never going to be a genius," says Taddy. "We don't believe that is true. Even if kids are growing up in a home where the mother cannot read to them, or there is no real mental stimulation. You need different methods. You can catch people up." The model works, says Taddy. You can build a university anywhere. Every now and again, he likes to head into the bush, to a place called Ezemvelo, about an hour from Johannesburg. The name means "return to nature", but it is more than a nature reserve; it is the eco-campus of the Maharishi Institute, where students come to learn about conservation, tourism, organic agriculture, alternative forms of energy. And at night, Taddy will look into the sky, just as he did when he was a little boy, and he will see them again, his friends, the bright and shining stars, symbols and messengers of the infinite possibility that dwells within us all.

What Makes a Social Enterprise Fail?

ocial enterprises operate in environments with an ingrained conflict between social and economic value, and Seanor and Meaton
(2007) highlight the roles played by the themes of ambiguity and trust
in organisational failure.

Ambiguity, they argue, causes a "lack of a single clear message, upon
which individuals can decide to act, or choose not to act" (2007, p. 28).
This ambiguity is both a hindrance, as it inhibits the growth of a strong
identity, and also a boon, as social enterprises benefit from the hybrid
model, shifting easily between the realms of voluntary, private and social
organisations as it suits them. But the authors suggest that ambiguity
is ultimately hurtful, causing a lack of identity, and undermining trust
in the organisation (Seanor & Meaton, 2007). Trust is important for
entities that operate in an ambiguous environment, and it is a primary
theme in the literature on social capital. It is the glue that connects communities and networks together around a common goal, for the common good (Seanor & Meaton, 2007). Quoting Fenton et al., Seanor and
Meaton (2007) argue that organisations that operate across sectors, with
blurred lines that test the values-base of the organisations – for example
shifting from altruism to business-like approaches – lose trust.

The interchangeable environment within which social enterprises operate is therefore inherently distrustful, *hindering* co-operation and best
practice (Seanor & Meaton, 2007). Trust within the organisation's internal and external networks is vital to the relationships needed to deliver
co-ordinated services and outcomes, but it cannot be *assumed* (Seanor &
Meaton, 2007).

The collapse of CIDA City Campus is an example of an internal breakdown in trust driven by a growing ambiguity on the values-based approach
of the organisation. The model shows how the tension between the social
and economic drivers of the organisation led to a fallout between the
CEO and the board, with CIDA losing its "hero" entrepreneur, who set
up a replica, rival institution, which continues today. Almost seven years
after Taddy left, CIDA applied for business rescue – an example of why
social value and its themes of trust and ambiguity cannot be ignored.

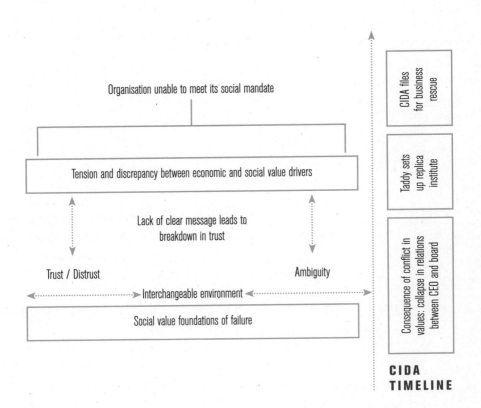

Organisation unable to meet its social mandate

Tension and discrepancy between economic and social value drivers

Lack of clear message leads to
breakdown in trust

Trust / Distrust

Ambiguity

Interchangeable environment

Social value foundations of failure

CIDA files for business rescue

Taddy sets up replica institute

Consequence of conflict in values: collapse in relations between CEO and board

CIDA TIMELINE

Social value failure within CIDA City Campus
Adapted from Seanor & Meaton, 2007

A GLOBAL PERSPECTIVE ON SOUTH AFRICAN SOCIAL ENTREPRENEURSHIP

A GLOBAL PERSPECTIVE ON SOUTH AFRICAN SOCIAL ENTREPRENEURSHIP

Jeffrey A. Robinson and Brett A. Gilbert
Rutgers Business School

It could be argued that there have always been social entrepreneurs. There have always been innovative people who have used their contacts, resources, and ingenuity to make their community better, to empower the disadvantaged and to make society a better place for all. However, in the 21st Century, we began to highlight and in some circles even to promote the idea of social entrepreneurship as a professional activity different from government and the public service, different from corporate social responsibility, and different from the world of NGOs and NPOs. The academic world began to take notice and the first papers, books, and courses emerged at colleges and universities around the world.

Given the social, political, and economic complexities of South Africa, it is no wonder that social entrepreneurship has emerged as a critical approach to address the inequalities that persist more than 20 years after the fall of apartheid. In fact, in 2002, Mandla Mentoor, creator of Soweto Mountain of Hope, was designated as one of the early Ashoka Fellows from South Africa. His work at the intersection of community development, environmental justice, and art was an incredible example of efforts that bridged the period at the end of apartheid with the beginning of a new era. When he began his work in 1990, he didn't rely on government or private enterprises to get things done; instead he organised local initiatives for young people to engage their community and to express their fears and dreams. People such as Mandla and those profiled in this book fascinate us because they embody the phenomenon of social entrepreneurship in its purest form.

In this chapter, we reflect on the 15 social entrepreneurs who are profiled in this book and position the lessons and insights from their work in the global conversation on social entrepreneurship that is occurring in universities, think tanks, government agencies, foundations and conferences on social and economic development. To organise our discussion, we examine the people and the process constituting social entrepreneurship.

The People

Who are the people responsible for the social entrepreneurship that is described in this book? Where do they come from? Why do they do what they do? These questions have been the focus of much of the literature written about social entrepreneurs. The authors of *The Power of Unreasonable People* speculate that social entrepreneurs do not consider the status quo to be a finality (Elkington & Hartigan, 2008). Reasonable people accept the status quo, whereas social entrepreneurs are unreasonable in the sense that they question it. This characteristic aptly describes several of the social entrepreneurs in this book. Jonathan Liebmann, Ludwick Marishane, Thandazile Mary Raletooane, and Yusuf Randera-Rees each endeavoured to change the status quo and are overcoming enormous challenges to do so. Liebmann is fighting against the "suburban" mentality of Johannesburg and seeking to create a township that connects people. Marishane, initially motivated by wanting to avoid the daily chore of bathing, invented a product that helps people who have no access to clean water to bathe using a moisturising gel. He has had to fight disbelief in the efficacy of the product. In Raletooane we see a woman fighting against the "neglect" for which her township is known and using that to spur the creation of a social, economic and political marketplace for sharing and engaging in value. Randera-Rees is similarly fighting to liberate entrepreneurs in their ideas and potential. Liebmann, Marishane, Raletooane, and Randera-Rees are this book's examples of "unreasonable people". They might also be described as "social constructionists" (Zahra, Gedajlovic, Neubaum, & Shulman, 2009).

This book provides examples of people whose compassion drove them to solve local problems in creative ways, consistent with Miller et al. who argue that a compassionate pro-social attitude is a powerful and important factor in the creation of new ventures (Miller, Grimes, McMullen, & Vogus, 2012). The case study of Garth Japhet illustrates a social venture that was founded through compassion. Japhet's passion for seeing people live healthier lives resulted in the creation of an educational series that shared positive health practices with the community. Zahra et al. would call people like Garth "social bricoleurs".

Research conducted by Germak and Robinson (2014) indicates that nascent social entrepreneurs either come from traditional business backgrounds or public-service and/or social-work backgrounds. These backgrounds precipitate several motivations for social entrepreneurs to start social ventures: personal fulfilment, helping society, non-monetary goals, achievement orientation, and closeness to social problems (2014, p. 19). The motivations are apparent in several cases in this book. Educators such as Pat Pillai and Sharanjeet Shan, the ideator Claire Reid, community developer Neil Campher, and school builders Stacey Brewer and Ryan Harrison, are fantastic examples of how people find different pathways to social entrepreneurship. The motivations of South African social entrepreneurs fit into the global conversations on why social entrepreneurs do what they do.

It is important to note that people from all sections of society must take up social entrepreneurship. The social entrepreneurs profiled in this book indeed come from diverse sectors of South Africa: black, white, coloured, and Indian. In true Rainbow Nation form, by profiling these individuals, South Africa is contributing to the global conversations taking place on the importance of diversity and access in social entrepreneurship. This conversation consists of two parts. First, all too often, the question of who is considered a social entrepreneur is more dependent on class, race/ethnicity and education than on who is doing the actual work in the communities. Second, the idea that social entrepreneurship can be democratic and disruptive belies the fact that many of the people who are promoted in social entrepreneurship don't look like the community members they serve. The point here is not to condemn people who want to do good work in disadvantaged communities. Rather, we acknowledge that more needs to be done to empower the local entrepreneur and community leader to use these new tools, language, and approaches so that everyone can tap into this global movement and the resources that are available to support social entrepreneurs.

The Process of Social Entrepreneurship

The case studies in this book clearly illustrate that social entrepreneurs are extraordinary people who do extraordinary things. However, if we want to teach others how to be social entrepreneurs we must have a more rigorous way of presenting the key elements of the process. Thus, the *process* of social entrepreneurship needs to be understood. In work that is more than a decade old, Robinson (2006) sought to understand how the process of social entrepreneurship unfolds for the social entrepreneur. According to Robinson, the process involves:

the identification of a specific social problem and a specific solution (or set of solutions) to address it; the evaluation of the social impact, the business model and the sustainability of the venture; and the creation of a social mission-oriented for-profit or a business-oriented non-profit entity that pursues the double (or triple) bottom line (Robinson, 2006, p. 95).

By defining social entrepreneurship as a process, we focus our insights on what social entrepreneurs actually do. In a more recent paper, Prado, Robinson and Shapira (2016) name four "elements" of social entrepreneurship: social impact, social innovation, financial sustainability, and measurement. The global conversation about the process of social entrepreneurship focuses on what we can learn from the best practitioners (Elkington & Hartigan, 2008), and we will therefore examine each of these elements in relation to South Africa's finest social entrepreneurs.

SOCIAL IMPACT

The first element of social entrepreneurship described by Prado, Robinson and Shapira (2016) is social impact, which every authentic social entrepreneur strives to make. Social entrepreneurs want to solve a problem, address an inequality, empower individuals or a community, reduce an environmental impact, or develop a mechanism for improving the quality of life of the people who live in a particular place (Mair, Robinson & Hockerts, 2006; Nicholls & Cho, 2006; Short, Moss & Lumpkin, 2009; Zahra et al., 2009). Social entrepreneurs are intent on having a social impact not as an afterthought but as an integral part of their business and operational model. This is in sharp contrast with CSI, through which corporations invest resources in activities that benefit society, but in which social impact is not the central mission or core activity of the company.

Each of the case studies in this book is an excellent example of how social entrepreneurs are motivated by an integral social mission. Randera-Rees wants to create more entrepreneurs who create wealth and transform the economy. Raletooane wants to change the economic outcomes of the disabled and disenfranchised. Liebmann wants to transform the inner-city from a place of despair into a place of economic opportunity. All of these social entrepreneurs want to make a difference in their communities and in the nation. These case studies provide us with many ways to conceive of the scale and scope of social impact in an emerging economy.

SOCIAL INNOVATION

The second element of social entrepreneurship described by Prado, Robinson and Shapira (2016) is social innovation, the new practices and approaches that are used to address social issues and environmental problems. Prado, Robinson and Shapira (2016) place these innovations into three categories.

Category 1: Innovation in business models that span the boundaries between what are typically thought of as government, social and private sectors.

An example of a social entrepreneur who demonstrates this category of social innovation is Raletooane, who created Itekeng Clean and Green as a venture that hires young people, disabled people, and parents of disabled people to "keep the streets clean and the environment green". This approach blurs the boundaries between government, social and private sector activities that are traditionally separate. In doing so, Raletooane created a marketplace that bridges the social, political and economic spheres and has a positive economic impact on the community.

Category 2: Service-delivery innovations that connect underserved people with appropriate resources.

Campher uses the Asset-Based Community Development approach to connect various community resources and people in Helenvale. These types of innovations emerge where government is not effective in delivering services to communities. Social entrepreneurs figure out ways to connect and organise local resources into empowering and effective projects and programmes.

Category 3: Technological innovations that are used to address social and environmental issues.

Marishane uses technology to address a social issue with DryBath, a product that enables people to bath without using water, allowing those who live in water-scarce areas to live healthier lives. Mueller et al. (2014) argue that we do not know as much as we should about the process of social innovation, and how to encourage more of it. How do we foster this type of innovative thinking so that it can be used to solve the most pressing problems in society? What are the pathways from social science to social entrepreneurship? As we consider South Africa and other emerging markets, these are important questions that the field is yet to answer.

FINANCIAL SUSTAINABILITY

The third element of social entrepreneurship described by Prado, Robinson and Shapira (2016) is financial sustainability. The most prevalent modes of fundraising for NGOs are donations and grants (Bugg-Levine & Emerson, 2011; Elkington & Hartigan, 2008). Governments raise funds for social initiatives from local and corporate tax bases. When social entrepreneurship is posed as an alternative to NGOs and government, financial sustainability is important in the long-term viability of these solutions.

The social entrepreneurs in this book have found creative ways to fund their activities so that they are not reliant on grants and donations. Gregory Maqoma, of Vuyani Dance Theatre, articulates this best when he says: "There were great and wonderful things we were doing, but they were not income-generating." Ventures that fail to generate income are forced to rely on beneficent donors and grant programmes. By charging for services, Maqoma reduced the dependency of his venture on donations by 60 per cent, stating that Vuyani is now "contributing to the economy...creating jobs with sustainability". The best social entrepreneurs figure out ways to be financially sustainable.

The global conversation on social entrepreneurship focuses not only on financially sustainable business models, but also on how to fund social ventures. Just as venture capitalists are interested in funding new ventures that will provide significant return on their investment, social-impact investors are interested in funding new ventures that have a positive social impact. In 2010, JP Morgan released a report in collaboration with the Rockefeller Foundation entitled "Impact Investing: A New Asset Class" that estimated that hundreds of millions of dollars will be invested in this new asset class (O'Donohoe, Leijonhufvud, Saltuk, Bugg-Levine & Brandenburg, 2010).

Impact investors are also emerging in South Africa. However, the majority of social entrepreneurs do not yet have scalable or sustainable business models and are therefore not ready to meet the demands of these new investors.

MEASUREMENT

The fourth element of social entrepreneurship identified by Prado, Robinson and Shapira (2016) is the measurement of social impact. Globally, the conversation on social-impact measurement lacks clarity. Therefore, it is not surprising that this conversation is not represented in the case studies in this book. Many social entrepreneurs focus on delivering valuable services and products before they consider measuring the success of their efforts. Measurement will become a central part of the discussion when impact investors try to evaluate existing investments or when they are comparing the relative impact of investing in venture A as opposed to venture B (Ebrahim & Rangan, 2011).

One of the leading voices in this conversation is the Global Impact Investment Network (www.thegiin.org). This network of impact investors and partners is interested in supporting the field of impact investing and in developing social-impact measurements. However, social-impact measurement is challenging, because comparison requires established, standardised methods. A recent *Academy of Management Review* article by Kroeger & Weber (2014) presents measuring and comparing social-value creation across multiple ventures or organisations as an idea that has many complications. It is not easy to understand how social impact can be accurately measured, taking all of the factors into account. This aspect of social entrepreneurship is emerging in the literature and in practice. As the global field continues to evolve in this area, impact investors will begin to fund ventures in South Africa and to ask social entrepreneurs to be more definitive about how they measure their social impact.

The Future of Social Entrepreneurship in South Africa

The case studies in this book leave us optimistic about the future of social entrepreneurship in South Africa. There will always be socially minded individuals, such as the social entrepreneurs profiled in these pages, who see social problems as challenges that need to be overcome, devise solutions that work, and figure out how to make them sustainable. As these extraordinary social entrepreneurs increase the scale of their solutions, we expect to see their impact across South Africa and beyond.

REFERENCES AND FURTHER READING

CHAPTERS AND INTERVIEWS

Dreaming and Disrupting:
The Power of Social Entrepreneurship

Ludwick Marishane: The Eureka Moment of Ludwick Marishane
Kermeliotis, T. (2014, March 10). "DryBath: How to Keep Clean without Using a Drop of Water". Retrieved 15 January 2016, from http://edition.cnn.com/2014/03/10/business/drybath-how-to-keep-clean/index.html
"Headboy Industries Inc.". (n.d.). Retrieved 15 January 2016, from www.headboy.org/drybath
Interview: L. Marishane, 11 March 2015
Marishane, L. (2012, December). "A Bath without Water". Retrieved 15 January 2016, from http://www.ted.com/talks/ludwick_marishane_a_bath_without_water
Sotunde, O. (2012, August 25). "Meet the World's Best Student Entrepreneur – Ventures Africa". Retrieved 15 January 2016, from http://venturesafrica.com/making-an-example-of-the-world's-best-student-entrepreneur/

Jonathan Liebmann: The Maverick of Maboneng
Interview: J. Liebmann, 17 February 2015
Liebmann, J. (2010, October). "Developing a Community Economy". Retrieved 15 January 2016, from http://www.youtube.com/watch?v=QjRvqwMOx-Q
"Maboneng: Home". (n.d.). Retrieved 15 January 2016, from http://www.mabonengprecinct.com/
Ogutu, R.K. (2013, November 9). "Diary of an Under 30 CEO: Turning Rubble into Riches – Ventures Africa". Retrieved 15 January 2016, from http://www.venturesafrica.com/diary-of-an-under-30-ceo-turning-rubble-into-riches

Thandazile Mary Raletooane: A Mother of the Nation in a Place of Neglect
Interview: T.M. Raletooane, 23 March 2015
"Red Bull Amaphiko Academy: Thandazile Mary Raletooane". (2014, June 9). Retrieved 15 January 2016, from https://www.youtube.com/watch?v=FfAAnRtjyC4
Raletooane, T.M. (2011). "Proposal for Funding to Tamara Trust". Retrieved 15 January 2016, from www.tamaratrust.org

Mind of the Maverick:
Personality Traits of Social Entrepreneurs

Yusuf Randera-Rees: A New Revolution on Constitution Hill
"The Awethu Project". (2016). Retrieved 15 January 2016, from http://www.awethuproject.co.za/about-awethu
"Yusuf Randera-Rees". (n.d.). Retrieved 15 January 2016, from http://crawfordschools.co.za/?p=2978
Interview: Y. Randera-Rees, 13 March 2015
"Awethu Project Helps Entrepreneurs". (2011, November 29). Retrieved 15 January 2016, from http://www.jda.org.za/news-and-media-releases-2011/november/774-awethu-project-helps-entrepreneurs
Randera-Rees, Y. (2011, March 17). "Exploring Unexplored Markets". TEDx Johannesburg Talk. Retrieved 15 January 2016, from http://www.youtube.com/watch?v=5_5x220uTP0

Garth Japhet: The Heart and Soul of Dr Garth Japhet
"Garth Japhet | Ashoka – Innovators for the Public". (2008). Retrieved 15 January 2016, from http://www.ashoka.org/fellow/garth-japhet
Interview: G. Japhet, 10 February 2015
"Soul City Institute for Health & Development Communication". (n.d.). Retrieved 15 January 2016, from http://www.soulcity.org.za/
"HEARTLINES". (n.d.). Retrieved 15 January 2016, from http://www.heartlines.org.za/
"#441 | Dr. Garth Japhet Interview | CEO of Heartlines". (n.d.). Retrieved 15 January 2016, from http://thelegacyproject.co.za/441-dr-garth-japhet-interview-ceo-of-heartlines/

Sharanjeet Shan: The Meaning of Love is Mathematics

Interview: S. Shan, 29 January 2015

"MCIS". (n.d.). Retrieved 15 January 2016, from http://www.mcis.org.za/

"Sharanjeet Shan". (n.d.). Retrieved 15 January 2016, from http://www.schwabfound.org/content/sharanjeet-shan

"Schwab Foundation – Sharanjeet Shan". (n.d.). Retrieved 15 January 2016, from http://www.schwabfound.org/content/sharanjeet-shan

Shan, S. (2015, September 25). "Mathematics has to be Taught with Love and Discipline". Retrieved 15 January 2016, from https://www.linkedin.com/pulse/mathematics-has-taught-love-discipline-sharanjeet-shan?trk=pulse-det-nav_art

Shan, S. (2015, September 1). "Schools a Missed Opportunity". Retrieved 15 January 2016, from https://www.linkedin.com/pulse/schools-missed-opportunity-sharanjeet-shan

Anne Githuku-Shongwe: A Game-Changer of the African Mind

"Afroes". (n.d.). Retrieved 15 January 2016, from http://afroes.com/

Githuku-Shongwe, A. (2013, May 6). "The Greatest Return of Investment is Investing in the Mindsets of the Future Generation of Leaders". Retrieved 1 January 2016, from http://www.huffingtonpost.com/anne-githukushongwe/afroes-anne-githuku-shongwe_b_2819045.html

Githuku-Shongwe, A. (2012, October 27). "Why I Quit My UN Job to Make Video Games". Daily Nation. Retrieved 15 January 2016, from www.nation.co.ke/lifestyle/saturday/Why-I-quit-my-UN-job-to-make-video-games/-/1216/1604142/-/view/printVersion/-/1hkmo3/-/index.html

Interview: A. Githuku-Shongwe, 17 March 2015

Schwab Foundation for Social Entrepreneurship. (n.d.). "Anne Githuku-Shongwe". Retrieved 15 January 2016, from www.schwabfound.org/content/anne-githuku-shongwe

Navigating the Great Unknown:
Strategies and Approaches of Social Entrepreneurs

SPARK Schools: SPARK of a Revolution

Brewer, S. (2011). "A Sustainable Financial Model for Low-Fee Private Schools in South Africa". Master of Business Administration Thesis, Gordon Institute of Business Science.

Brewer, S. & Harrison, R. (n.d.). "Christensen Institute – Spark Schools". Retrieved 15 January 2016, from http://www.christensen-institute.org/spark-schools

Dutta, S., Geiger, T. & Lanvin, B. (2015). "The Global Information Technology Report 2015". Retrieved 15 January 2016, from www.weforum.org/reports/global-information-technology-report-2015

"EAdvance – The Future of Education in South Africa". (n.d.). Retrieved 15 January 2016, from http://www.eadvance.co.za/

"Fanning the Flames: Spark Schools Joins ISASA". (2014, March 17). Retrieved 15 January 2016, from http://www.ieducation.co.za/category/featured/page/5/

Interview: S. Brewer & R. Harrison, 2 February 2015

"Home – SPARK Schools". (n.d.). Retrieved 15 January 2016, from http://www.sparkschools.co.za/

Wilkinson, K. (2015, March 25). "Checked: 80% of South African Schools Indeed 'Dysfunctional'". Retrieved 15 January 2016, from http://mg.co.za/article/2015-03-25-are-80-of-south-african-schools-dysfunctional/

Neil Campher: Turning Waste into Worth in Helenvale

Interview: N. Campher, 20 July 2015

Lundahl, E. & Södergren, N. (2008). "Township Upgrading of Helenvale". Master of Spatial Planning Thesis, Blekinge Institute of Technology. Retrieved 15 January 2016, from www.diva-portal.se/smash/get/diva2:829988/FULLTEXT01.pdf

Mandela Bay Development Agency. (2014, May). "Mandela Bay Development Agency: 2009–2013 Economic Barometer". Retrieved 15 January 2016, from www.mbda.co.za/MBDA/Media/872014124048.pdf

Reos Partners. (n.d.). "Live, Learn, Work, Pray: The North Star Scenarios". Retrieved 15 January 2016, from www.reospartners.com

Pat Pillai: Life is a Teacher

Interview: P. Pillai, 25 February 2015

"Patmanathan Pillai | Ashoka – Innovators for the Public". (n.d.). Retrieved 15 January 2016, from www.ashoka.org/fellow/patmanathan-pillai

"LifeCo UnLtd South Africa". (n.d.). Retrieved 15 January 2016, from www.lcu-sa.com

Modise, T. (2015, May 22). "Pat Pillai: 'Entrepreneurship is a State of Mind'". Retrieved 15 January 2016, from www.fin24.com/BizNews/Pat-Pillai-Entrepreneurship-is-a-state-of-mind-20150522

Gregory Maqoma: The Man Who Dances for Joy

Interview: G. Maqoma, 18 February 2015

Kodesh, H. (2008). "Chapter One: A South African Cultural Cocktail". Retrieved 15 January 2016, from http://wiredspace.wits.ac.za/bitstream/handle/10539/4719/9.%20chap%201%20cultural%20cocktail.pdf?sequence=9

Piedade, J.S. (2010, May 24). "The Syncretisms of Gregory Maqoma: BUALA African Contemporary Culture". Retrieved 15 January 2016, from http://mappinternational.org/files/rf4f0cadc941774/Full%20Press%20Reviews.pdf

"Vuyani Dance Company Website". (n.d.). Retrieved 15 January 2016, from www.vuyani.co.za

Claire Reid: The Business that Grew in a Garden

CNBC Africa. (2010, December 15). "Eureka – Reel Gardening Invented by Claire Reid". Retrieved 15 January 2016, from www.youtube.com/watch?v=AlYqhfrzDEM

Interview: C. Reid, 11 February 2015

"Reel Gardening". (n.d.). Retrieved 15 January 2016, from www.reel-gardening.co.za

Reid, C. (2013, December 6). "Growing Your Own Food, Easy as 1 2 3". TEDxJohannesburgWomen Talk. Retrieved 15 January 2016, from www.youtube.com/watch?v=VdITNg8qydc

Kovin Naidoo: A Man of Radical Vision

"Brien Holden Vision Institute". (n.d.). Retrieved 15 January 2016, from www.brienholdenvision.org

Interview: K. Naidoo, 10 March 2015

Naidoo, K. (2000). "Towards a New Model of Optometry". The Journal of Optometric Education, 25(2)

Schwab Foundation for Social Entrepreneurship. (n.d.). "Kovin Naidoo". Retrieved 15 January 2016, from www.schwabfound.org/content/kovin-naidoo

World Council of Optometry. (2005, April 1). "World Optometry: Enhancing Vision, Protecting Health – A Case Study". Retrieved 15 January 2016, from www.worldoptometry.org/download.cfm/docid/74E80E5A-B15A-4BD2-AB493E163492EC2C

Taddy Blecher: An Alchemist of Human Potential

Cook, M.J. (2014, February 21). "Blecher Changes the Education Paradigm". Media Club South Africa. Retrieved 15 January 2016, from www.mediaclubsouthafrica.com/land-and-people/3717-blecher-changes-the-education-paradigm#ixzz3pPhUcede

Interview: T. Blecher, 18 February 2015

"Maharishi Institute Website". (n.d.). Retrieved 15 January 2016, from www.maharishiinstitute.org

The Economist. (2007, August 30). "The Transcendental Crusader". Retrieved 15 January 2016, from www.economist.com/node/9723263

World Business Academy. (2005, June 23). "A South African Social Entrepreneur Turns a New Economic Vision into Practice". Retrieved 15 January 2016, from www.worldbusiness.org/wp-content/uploads/2013/06/mv062305.pdf

Academic Sections and Additional Reading

Austin, J., Stevenson, H. & Wei-Skillern, J. (2006). "Social and Commercial Entrepreneurship: Same, Different or Both?" Entrepreneurship Theory and Practice, 30(1), 1–22. Retrieved 13 December 2015, from http://doi.org/10.1111/j.1540-6520.2006.00107.x

Bloom, P.N. & Smith, B.R. (2010). "Identifying the Drivers of Social Entrepreneurial Impact: Theoretical Development and an Exploratory Empirical Test of SCALERS". Journal of Social Entrepreneurship, 1(1), 126–145. Retrieved 13 December 2015, from http://doi.org/10.1080/19420670903458042

Bremner, L. (2000). "Reinventing the Johannesburg Inner City".

Cities, 17(3), 185–193. Retrieved 13 December 2015, from http://doi.org/10.1016/S0264-2751(00)00013-5

Bugg-Levine, A. & Emerson, J. (2011). "Impact Investing: Transforming How We Make Money while Making a Difference". Innovations, 6(3), 9–18

Bull, M. (2009). "Challenging Tensions: Critical, Theoretical and Empirical Perspectives on Social Enterprise". Retrieved 13 December 2015, from http://doi.org/10.1108/13552550810897641

Chell, E. (2000). "Towards Researching the Opportunistic Entrepreneur: A Social Constructionist Approach and Research Agenda". European Journal of Work and Organizational Psychology, 9 February 2015, 63–80. Retrieved 13 December 2015, from http://doi.org/10.1080/135943200398067

Chell, E. (2007). "Social Enterprise and Entrepreneurship: Towards a Convergent Theory of the Entrepreneurial Process". International Small Business Journal, 25(1), 5–26. Retrieved 13 December 2015, from http://doi.org/10.1177/0266242607071779

Chell, E., Nicolopoulou, K. & Karatas-Ozkan, M. (2010). "Social Entrepreneurship and Enterprise: International and Innovation Perspectives". Entrepreneurship & Regional Development, 22(6), 485–493. Retrieved 13 December 2015, from http://doi.org/10.1080/08985626.2010.488396

Cheng, P., Goodall, E., Hodgkinson, R. & Kingston, J. (2010). Financing the Big Society: Why Social Investment Matters. Kent

Christopoulos, D. & Vogl, S. (2014). "The Motivation of Social Entrepreneurs: The Roles, Agendas and Relations of Altruistic Economic Actors". Journal of Social Entrepreneurship, 6(1), 1–30. Retrieved 13 December 2015, from http://doi.org/10.1080/19420676.2014.954254

Corner, P.D. & Ho, M. (2010). "How Opportunities Develop in Social Entrepreneurship". Entrepreneurship Theory and Practice, 34(4), 635–659. Retrieved 13 December 2015, from http://doi.org/10.1111/j.1540-6520.2010.00382.x

Dakoumi, A.H. & Abdelwahed, Y. (2014). "Is Entrepreneurship for You? Effects of Storytelling on Entrepreneurial Intention". International Journal of Business and Management, 9(9), 176–192. Retrieved 13 December 2015, from http://doi.org/10.5539/ijbm.v9n9p176

Dees, J.G. (2001). "The Meaning of Social Entrepreneurship", 1–5

Dees, J.G. & Anderson, B. (2003). "For-Profit Social Ventures". International Journal of Entrepreneurship Education, 2(1), 1–26. Retrieved 18 January 2016, from http://catcher.sandiego.edu/items/soles/DeesAndersonCase.pdf

Defourny, J. & Nyssens, M. (2010). "Conceptions of Social Enterprise and Social Entrepreneurship in Europe and the United States: Convergences and Divergences". Journal of Social Entrepreneurship, 1(1), 32–53. Retrieved 13 December 2015, from http://doi.org/10.1080/19420670903442053

Di Domenico, M., Haugh, H. & Tracey, P. (2010). "Social Bricolage: Theorizing Social Value Creation in Social Enterprises". Entrepreneurship Theory and Practice, 34(4), 681–703. Retrieved 13 December 2015, from http://doi.org/10.1111/j.1540-6520.2010.00370.x

Drakopoulou Dodd, S. & Anderson, A.R. (2007). "Mumpsimus and the Mything of the Individualistic Entrepreneur". International Small Business Journal, 25(4), 341–360. Retrieved 13 December 2015, from http://doi.org/10.1177/0266242607078561

Drucker, P.F. (1998). "The Discipline of Innovation". Harvard Business Review, 80(8), 328–336. Retrieved 13 December 2016, from https://hbr.org/2002/08/the-discipline-of-innovation

Drucker, P. (2005). Managing the Nonprofit Organisation: Practices and Principles. New York: Harper

Ebrahim, A. & Rangan, V.K. (2011). "Acumen Fund: Measurement in Impact Investing (A)". Boston: Harvard Business School Publishing

Elkington, J. & Hartigan, P. (2008). The Power of Unreasonable People: How Social Entrepreneurs Create Markets that Change the World. Boston: Harvard Business School Publishing

Fletcher, D.E. (2006). "Entrepreneurial Processes and the Social Construction of Opportunity". Entrepreneurship & Regional Development, 18(5), 421–440. Retrieved 13 December 2015, from http://doi.org/10.1080/08985620600861105

Germak, A.J. & Robinson, J.A. (2014). "Exploring the Motivation of Nascent Social Entrepreneurs". Journal of Social Entrepreneurship, 5(1), 5–21. Retrieved 13 December 2015, from http://doi.org/10.1080/19420676.2013.820781

Greve, A. & Salaff, J.W. (2003). "Social Networks and Entrepreneurship". ET&P, (28), 1–22. doi:10.1111/1540-8520.00029

Jones, G. (2013). "Lesson in Business Admin". Financial Mail.

Retrieved 13 December 2015, from www.financialmail.co.za/business/fox/2013/05/09/lesson-in-business-admin

Kickul, J. & Lyons, T.S. (2012). Understanding Social Entrepreneurship: The Relentless Pursuit of Mission in an Ever Changing World. New York: Routledge

Kickul, J. & Lyons, T.S. (2013). "The Social Enterprise Financing Landscape: The Lay of the Land and New Research on the Horizon". Entrepreneurship Research Journal, 3(2), 147–159.

Koe, J., Nga, H. & Shamuganathan, G. (2010). "The Influence of Personality Traits and Demographic Factors on Social Entrepreneurship Start Up Intentions". Journal of Business Ethics, 95(2), 259–282. Retrieved 13 December 2015, from http://doi.org/10.1007/s10551-009-0358-8

Krige, K. (2015). "The Governance, Leadership and Funding Commonalities of Ten Civil Society Organisations that have Thrived in a Constrained Environment". Master of Development Studies Thesis, University of KwaZulu-Natal

Krige, K. (2016). "A Discussion on Social Entrepreneurship in South Africa: A Look at Why Social Entrepreneurship Offers Opportunity to Strengthen Civil Society and Fast Track Socio-Economic Development in South Africa" in Fields, D.Z. (Ed.). (2015). Incorporating Business Models and Strategies into Social Entrepreneurship. 292–312. Hershey: IGI Global

Kroeger, A. & Weber, C. (2014). "Developing a Conceptual Framework for Comparing Social Value Creation". Academy of Management Review, 39(4), 513–540

Lyon, F. & Fernandez, H. (2012). "Strategies for Scaling up Social Enterprise: Lessons from Early Years Providers". Social Enterprise Journal, 8(1), 63–77. Retrieved 13 December 2015, from http://doi.org/10.1108/17508611211226593

Lyon, F. & Sepulveda, L. (2009). "Mapping Social Enterprises: Past Approaches, Challenges and Future Directions". Social Enterprise Journal, 5(1), 83–94. Retrieved 13 December 2015, from http://doi.org/10.1108/17508610910956426

Maclean, M., Harvey, C. & Gordon, J. (2013). "Social Innovation, Social Entrepreneurship and the Practice of Contemporary Entrepreneurial Philanthropy". International Small Business Journal, 31(7), 747–763. Retrieved 13 December 2015, from http://doi.org/10.1177/0266242612443376

Maclean, M., Harvey, C., Gordon, J. & Shaw, E. (2015). "Identity, Storytelling and the Philanthropic Journey". Human Relations, 68(10), 1623–1652. Retrieved 13 December 2015, from http://doi. org/10.1177/0018726714564199

Mair, J. (2010). "Social Entrepreneurship: Taking Stock and Looking Ahead". No. WP-888. Barcelona: IESE Business School. Retrieved 13 December 2015, from http://www.world-entrepreneurship-forum. com/2010/index.php/content/download/1696/39638/version/2/file/ Mair_Social Entrepreneurship.pdf

Mair, J. & Noboa, E. (2003). "Social Entrepreneurship: How Intentions to Create a Social Enterprise Get Formed". Working Paper No. D/521. Barcelona: IESE Business School. Retrieved 13 December 2015, from http://dx.doi.org/10.2139/ssrn.462283

Mair, J., Robinson, J.A. & Hockerts, K. (2006). Social Entrepreneurship. London: Palgrave

"Mandla Mentoor | Ashoka – Innovators for the Public". (2002). Retrieved 9 February 2016, from https://www.ashoka.org/fellow/ mandla-mentoor

Mathie, A. & Cunningham, G. (2003). "Who is Driving Development? Reflections on the Transformative Potential of Asset Based Community Development". COADY International Institute: Occasional Paper Series, (5)

McLoughlin, J., Kaminski, J., Sodagar, B., Khan, S., Harris, R., Arnaudo, G. & McBrearty, S. (2009). "A Strategic Approach to Social Impact Measurement of Social Enterprises". Social Enterprise Journal, 5(2), 154–178. Retrieved 13 December 2015, from http:// doi.org/10.1108/17508610910981734

Miller, T.L., Grimes, M.G., McMullen, J.S. & Vogus, T.J. (2012). "Venturing for Others with Heart and Head: How Compassion Encourages Social Entrepreneurship". Academy of Management Review, 37(4), 616–640

Mueller, S., D'Intino, R.S., Walske, J., Ehrenhard, M.L., Newbert, S.L., Robinson, J.A. & Senjem, J.C. (2014). "What's Holding Back Social Entrepreneurship? Removing the Impediments to Theoretical Advancement". Journal of Social Entrepreneurship (forthcoming publication), 1–12

Nicholls, A. (Ed.). (2008). Social Entrepreneurship: New Models of Sustainable Change. Oxford: Oxford University Press

Nicholls, A. & Cho, A.H. (2006). "Social Entrepreneurship: The

Structuration of a Field" in Nicholls, A. (Ed.). (2008). Social
Entrepreneurship: New Models of Sustainable Social Change.
Oxford: Oxford University Press, 99–118

O'Donohoe, N., Leijonhufvud, C., Saltuk, Y., Bugg-Levine, A.
& Brandenburg, M. (2010). Impact Investments: An Emerging
Asset Class. New York: Rockefeller Foundation & Global Impact
Investment Network

Parker, S.C. (2014). "Who Become Serial and Portfolio Entrepreneurs?"
Small Business Economics, 43(4), 887–898. Retrieved 13 December
2015, from http://doi.org/10.1007/s11187-014-9576-2

Perrini, F., Vurro, C. & Costanzo, L.A. (2010). "A Process-Based
View of Social Entrepreneurship: From Opportunity Identification
to Scaling-Up Social Change in the Case of San Patrignano".
Entrepreneurship & Regional Development, 22(6), 515–534.
Retrieved 13 December 2015, from http://doi.org/10.1080/08985626
.2010.488402

Plehn-Dujowich, J. (2010). "A Theory of Serial Entrepreneurship".
Small Business Economics, 35(4), 377–398. Retrieved 13 December
2015, from http://doi.org/10.1007/s11187-008-9171-5

Prado, A., Robinson, J.A. & Shapira, Z. (2016). "Creating Social
and Economic Value at the Base of the Pyramid: A Social
Entrepreneurship Approach ". Working Paper. Costa Rica: INCAE
Business School

Rivera-Santos, M., Holt, D., Littlewood, D. & Kolk, A. (2014). "Social
Entrepreneurship in Sub-Saharan Africa". Academy of Management
Perspectives, 29 (1), 72–91. doi:10.1177/0007650315613293

Robinson, J. (2006). "Navigating Social and Institutional Barriers
to Markets: How Social Entrepreneurs Identify and Evaluate
Opportunities" in Mair, J., Robinson, J.A. & Hockerts, K. (Eds.).
(2006). Social Entrepreneurship. London: Palgrave

Sandu, C. & Haines, R. (2014). "Theory of Governance and
Social Enterprise". The USV Annals of Economics and Public
Administration, 14(2), 204–222

Santos, F.M. (2012). "A Positive Theory of Social Entrepreneurship".
Journal of Business Ethics, 111(3), 335–351. Retrieved 13 December
2015, from http://doi.org/10.1007/s10551-012-1413-4

Schwab, K., Sala-i-Martin, X., Eide, E.B. & Blanke, J. (2014). Global
Competitiveness Report – South Africa (Vol. 1). Geneva: World
Economic Forum

Schwandt, D.R., Holliday, S. & Pandit, G. (2009). "The Complexity of Social Entrepreneurship Systems: Social Change by the Collective" in Hazy, J. and Goldstein, J. (Eds.). (2009). Complexity and Social Entrepreneurship. NC: Information Age Publishing. Retrieved 13 December 2015, from http://www.scotholliday.com/uploads/2/9/5/2/2952155/schwandt_holliday_and_pandit-_book_chapter-_sept_2009-_the_complexity_of_social_entrepreneurship_systems.pdf

Seanor, P. & Meaton, J. (2007). "Learning from Failure, Ambiguity and Trust in Social Enterprise". Social Enterprise Journal, 4(1), 24–40. Retrieved 13 December 2015, from http://doi.org/10.1108/17508610810877713

Short, J., Moss, T.W. & Lumpkin, G.T. (2009). "Research in Social Entrepreneurship: Past Contributions and Future Opportunities". Strategic Entrepreneruship Journal, 3(2), 161–194

Smith, B.R. & Stevens, C.E. (2010). "Different Types of Social Entrepreneurship: The Role of Geography and Embeddedness on the Measurement and Scaling of Social Value". Entrepreneurship & Regional Development, 22(6), 575–598. Retrieved 13 December 2015, from http://doi.org/10.1080/08985626.2010.488405

Smith, W.K., Gonin, M. & Besharov, M.L. (2013). "Managing Social-Business Tensions". Business Ethics Quarterly, 23(3), 407–442. Retrieved 13 December 2015, from http://doi.org/10.5840/beq201323327

Sud, M., Vansandt, C.V. & Baugous, A.M. (2009). "Social Entrepreneurship: The Role of Institutions". Journal of Business Ethics, 85(Suppl. 1), 201–216. Retrieved 13 December 2015, from http://doi.org/10.1007/s10551-008-9939-1

Sunley, P. & Pinch, S. (2012). "Financing Social Enterprise: Social Bricolage or Evolutionary Entrepreneurialism?" Social Enterprise Journal, 8(2), 108–122. Retrieved 13 December 2015, from http://doi.org/10.1108/17508611211252837

Swanson, L.A. & Zhang, D.D. (2011). "Complexity Theory and the Social Entrepreneurship Zone". Emergence: Complexity & Organization, 13(3), 39–56

Teasdale, S. (2012). "What's in a Name? Making Sense of Social Enterprise Discourses". Public Policy and Administration, 27(2), 99–119. Retrieved 13 December 2015, from http://doi.org/10.1177/0952076711401466

Thompson, J., Alvy, G. & Lees, A. (2000). "Social Entrepreneurship: A New Look at the People and the Potential". Management Decision, 38(5), 328–338. Retrieved 13 December 2015, from http://doi.org/10.1108/00251740010340517

Thurston, S., Chakraborty, N.M., Hayes, B., Mackay, A. & Moon, P. (2015). "Establishing and Scaling-Up Clinical Social Franchise Networks: Lessons Learned from Marie Stopes International and Population Services International". Global Health, Science and Practice, 3(2), 180–194. Retrieved 13 December 2015, from http://doi.org/10.9745/GHSP-D-15-00057

Wallace, S.L. (1999). "Social Entrepreneurship: The Role of Social Purpose Enterprises in Facilitating Community Economic Development". Journal of Developmental Entrepreneurship, 4, 153–174

Weber, C., Kröger, A. & Lambrich, K. (2012). "Scaling Social Enterprises: A Theoretically Grounded Framework". Frontiers of Entrepreneurship Research, 32(19), Article 3

Wesley, F., Zimmerman, B. & Patton, M.Q. (2007). Getting to Maybe. Toronto: Vintage Canada

Westhead, P., Ucbasaran, D., Wright, M. & Binks, M. (2005). "Novice, Serial and Portfolio Entrepreneur Behaviour and Contributions". Small Business Economics, 25(2), 109–132. Retrieved 13 December 2015, from http://doi.org/10.1007/s11187-003-6461-9

World Economic Forum. (2006). "Blended Value Investing: Capital Opportunities for Social and Environmental Impact". 1–78. Retrieved 18 January 2015, from www.socialimpactexchange.org/sites/www.socialimpactexchange.org/files/publications/blended_value.pdf

World Health Organization. (2013). "South Africa: World Health Organization Statistical Profile 2013". Retrieved 15 January 2016, from www.who.int/countries/zaf/en/

Zahra, S.A., Gedajlovic, E., Neubaum, D.O. & Shulman, J.M. (2009). "A Typology of Social Entrepreneurs: Motives, Search Processes and Ethical Challenges". Journal of Business Venturing, 24(5), 519–532. Retrieved 13 December 2015, from http://doi.org/10.1016/j.jbusvent.2008.04.007

ACKNOWLEDGEMENTS

This book began as an idea and has become a reality thanks to the close involvement and passion of a small group of people.

The National Treasury and the Government of Flanders, whose commitment to social enterprise meant they didn't flinch at the idea of a book on a topic few people understood. Without their financial support and belief in our work, this book would have remained an idea.

The team at the GIBS Centre for Leadership and Dialogue led by Shireen Chengadu, who have experienced the ups and downs of book writing and production with us, and have always been on hand with advice, support and red-velvet cake. An enormous thank you.

Everything starts with an idea, and this book's origins belong to Itumeleng Dhlamini, who has that rare gift of making ideas happen. Thanks also to Kate Taylor, who kept us grounded and motivated with thoughtful solutions to tricky problems. To my other half, Ian, for patiently listening through the frustration and euphoria of producing a book over the year and a half it has taken to come to life.

But great ideas need management, and if it wasn't for Kovashni Gordhan and Russell Clarke holding the processes together – gently nudging Gus and I when we missed deadlines, allowing us to debate jacket covers when we were supposed to be printing – the book would have fallen. These pages are an example of how great ideas happen because of excellent teamwork, and Kovash and Russell were at the helm. To the team that assembled the book itself, our editor Wesley Thompson and designer extraordinaire Marius Roux, thank you for having the patience and grace of saints.

A special thank you to the peer reviewers for their feedback and comments that have contributed towards making this book soundly argued and comprehensive: Dr Alex Antonites, University of Pretoria; and Dr Ziska Fields, University of KwaZulu-Natal.

Thank you also to the Rutgers University team, Dr Jeffrey Robinson and Dr Brett Gilbert who, despite odd-hour Skype calls and emails, remained committed. Their chapter is a wonderful example of great academic thinking and writing.

We would like to thank our pioneers Gwen Ansell and Gretchen Wilson-Prangley for their support and ideas in the early days; and to our research team, Carmen Mollmann, Amie Burnett and Merith Read, for loving every interview, meticulously recording and transcribing them, and sharing their a-ha moments along the way.

Finally, we would like to thank all the social entrepreneurs profiled in this book – for accepting our invitation, for taking time out of your schedules for interviews, and for accommodating the additional questions and requests. Your stories are truly inspirational and we continue to learn from you.

Kerryn Krige
Gus Silber

NOTES ON METHOD

The social entrepreneurs profiled in this book were selected following a rigorous scan of the South African environment. Between the Network of Social Entrepreneurs database and adverts placed on Sangonet, we identified 1,500 socially focused organisations. From there, we carefully whittled out the non-profits and social-purpose businesses based on their organisational structure, their financial model, the intensity of their social mission, and the nature of their story. We selected the social entrepreneurs profiled in this book for the lessons that we could learn from them, and the questions they would leave us with: from the governance fall-out at CIDA, to the serial entrepreneurship of Garth Japhet, to the debate on Jonathan Liebmann's status as a social entrepreneur. We plotted them on the for-profit/not-for-profit spectrum to ensure we had a diversity of organisations and approaches. In order to extend our exposure of social entrepreneurship outside the urban areas of South Africa, we also profiled social entrepreneurs from the Free State, KwaZulu-Natal and Limpopo.

We conducted two-hour face-to-face interviews with the selected social entrepreneurs. The interviews were recorded and transcribed, and these materials are available on our website at www.leadingchange.co.za.

Gus Silber is our storyteller, working from each interview transcript and adding colour through extensive online research and follow-up telephone calls. Each social entrepreneur proofed their chapter, and we implemented their changes.

The academic sections at the end of each chapter are drawn from literature that gives insight into the South African context — it is not always the most up-to-date literature, but in this transformative space, it is relevant.

Rutgers University provided the conclusion, reviewing all of the chapters, drawing on knowledge generated from the South African context and adding their international perspective. This happened in tandem with the peer-review process, which provided valuable input on the teaching and academic value of the book.

This is by no means a comprehensive list of social entrepreneurs in South Africa, but it is an excellent starting point to understanding what social entrepreneurship looks like, and what drives these disruptors of business and society.

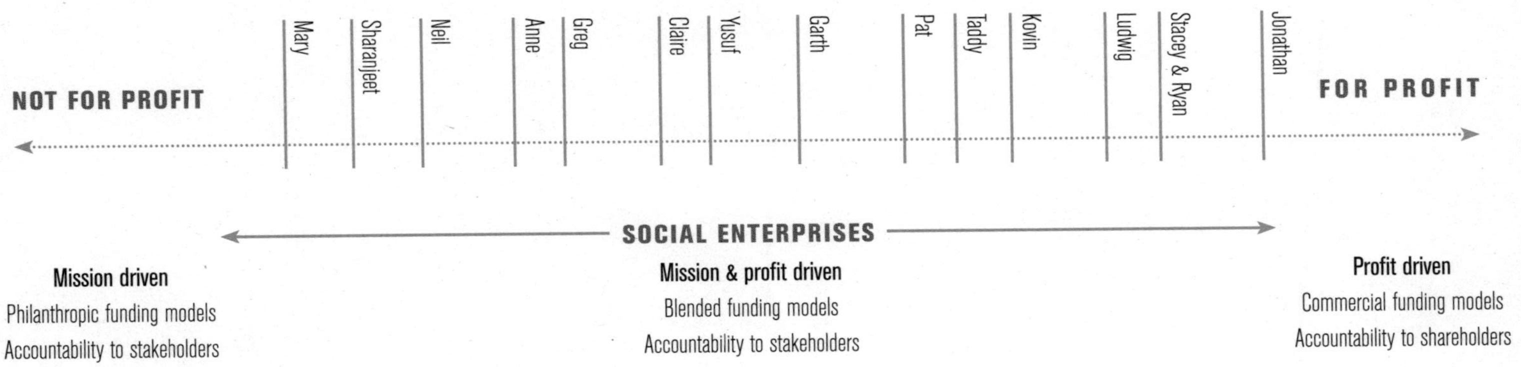

FOR PROFIT

Jonathan

Stacey & Ryan

Ludwig

Kovin

Taddy

Pat

Garth

Yusuf

Claire

Greg

Anne

Neil

Sharanjeet

Mary

NOT FOR PROFIT

SOCIAL ENTERPRISES

Profit driven
Commercial funding models
Accountability to shareholders

Mission & profit driven
Blended funding models
Accountability to stakeholders

Mission driven
Philanthropic funding models
Accountability to stakeholders

Research method: plotting our social entrepreneurs on the for-profit / not-for-profit spectrum
Based on Cheng et al, 2010